Painting & Wallcovering Techniques

Complete Handyman's Library™
Handyman Club of America
Minneapolis, Minnesota

Published in 1996 by
Handyman Club of America
12301 Whitewater Drive
Minnetonka, Minnesota 55343

Published by arrangement with Cowles Creative Publishing
ISBN 0-86573-663-4

Printed on American paper by
R. R. Donnelley & Sons Co.
99 98 97 96 / 5 4 3 2 1

CREDITS:
Created by: The Editors of Cowles Creative Publishing
and the staff of the Handyman Club of America
in cooperation with Black & Decker. **BLACK&DECKER**
is a trademark of Black & Decker (US), Incorporated
and is used under license.

Handyman Club of America:
    Vice President for Product Development: Mike Vail
    Book Marketing Director: Cal Franklin
    Book Products Development Manager: Steve Perlstein
    Book Marketing Coordinator: Jay McNaughton

Contents

Introduction

The colors, patterns, and textures you choose for your walls and ceilings are the final touches that bring to life any remodeling project. They create the ambience that makes each room a delightful setting. *Painting & Wallcovering Techniques* shows you simple techniques for expert painting and wallcovering that will help you fashion a beautiful room or an entire home.

The first section, "Room Design," will help you visualize how different combinations of color, pattern, and texture affect a room by showing you the same room as it changes "mood." This information will help you choose combinations for your projects that will reflect your taste and lifestyle.

Next, "Preparation" shows you how to prepare a project area. It demonstrates the latest methods and materials for repairing wallboard and plaster, and how to make surfaces ready for painting or wallcovering. It also includes advice on when and how to use primers and sealers.

The section on "Painting" covers all essential techniques for making beautiful finished surfaces. You learn how to estimate the proper amount of paint for a project, how to choose the right kind of paint, and how to apply it on walls, ceilings, and woodwork. This section also includes tips on painting safety, efficient cleanup, and how to safely dispose of paint materials.

The following section, "Wallcovering," in addition to containing basic measuring and installation techniques, shows you how to hang wallcovering on ceilings, how to get around obstacles like radiators and pipes, and how to wallcover switch and receptacle coverplates, recessed windows, and round archways.

Finally, "Decorative Painting" shows how to create an amazing array of unique painted surfaces. You'll learn techniques for stenciling, rag rolling, sponge painting, color washing, making faux marble or granite, and other special treatments. These techniques will work on walls, woodwork, furniture, and other room accessories.

Painting & Wallcovering Techniques contains everything you need to know, from how to choose paint and wallcoverings, to which tools to use and how to use them. The complete step-by-step instructions will guide you successfully through every phase of your project, including how to work safely and neatly.

Room Design

Color Basics

A new color scheme can dramatically change a room or your entire home. Even without changing expensive furniture or carpeting, a fresh infusion of color can transform the most ordinary room into an inviting living space.

Since color is a very personal choice, start your decorating scheme with colors you enjoy, such as those in your clothing, furnishings or artwork. Look for ideas in magazines. Browse decorating centers for paint colors, wallcoverings and fabric. Look at paint and wallcovering samples in your own home, using the 24-hour test. Color can look significantly different, depending on the lighting conditions and the surroundings.

Colors can be light or dark, warm or cool, bright or subdued. A color scheme sets the mood for the room, so choose colors that create the feeling you desire.

Glossary of Color Terms

Accent Color: A contrasting hue used to add visual interest in a color scheme

Color Scheme: A group of colors used together to create a mood or effect

Complementary Colors: Two colors directly opposite one another on the color wheel

Complementary Color Scheme: The use of complementary colors in a decorating plan

Contrasting Colors: Colors that have at least three other colors between them on tho oolor whool

Cool Colors: Blues, greens, purples

Desaturated Colors: Subdued hues; colors made less brilliant by the addition of white, black or complementary color

Hue: A color

Neutral Colors: Subtle variations of whites, grays, beiges

Primary Colors: Red, yellow and blue

Related Colors: Two colors next to one another on the color wheel

Related Color Scheme: The use of related colors in a decorating plan

Saturated Colors: Bright hues; intense colors undiluted by black, white or complementary color

Secondary Colors: Orange, green and purple; colors formed by mixing two primary colors

Shade: A darker hue variation, created by adding black or gray

Single-color Scheme: The use of varying shades of a single hue in a decorating plan

Tint: A lighter hue variation, created by adding white

Value: The scale of lightness or darkness of a color

Warm Colors: Reds, oranges, yellows and browns

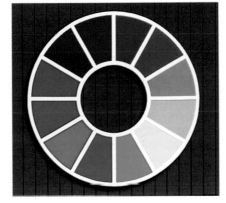

The color wheel shows how colors are related. Red, yellow and blue are primary colors. Orange, green and purple are secondary colors made by combining two primary colors. All colors are made from some combination of white, black and primary colors.

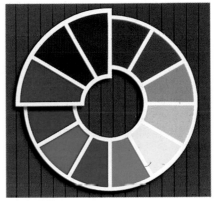

Related colors are those next to one another on the color wheel. Designers often build color schemes around two or three related colors.

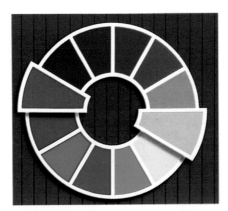

Complementary colors are located opposite each other on the color wheel. Blue, for example, is the complement of orange. Complementary colors enhance each other in decorating schemes.

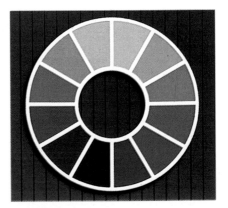

Neutral colors are shades of white, gray or beige. Most neutrals are tinted slightly with a warm or cool color. Neutral-colored walls provide a backdrop that does not compete with furnishings and accessories.

Light Colors

Light colors create bright, spacious rooms. To the eye, light colors seem to recede, making rooms appear larger and ceilings higher. Since light colors reflect the most light, they can brighten a north-facing room, a closet or dark hallway.

Whites and other light colors are good choices for a nursery or child's bedroom. In any room, white walls form a neutral background that does not compete with furnishings.

Wall roughness and paint sheen can affect the lightness of any color. Smooth surfaces and gloss paints reflect maximum light to make a color seem lighter. Rough-textured walls and flat-sheen paints hold more shadow and minimize the lightness of a color.

Light colors reflect light, which makes rooms appear larger and more open. In these rooms, the light furnishings blend with the walls to increase the open feeling. Use light wall colors in small rooms or in rooms with little natural light. Light colors help brighten a nursery or child's bedroom.

Dark Colors

Use dark colors to create an intimate room. Because dark colors absorb light, walls appear closer to make the room seem smaller. Dark colors are most often used in libraries, studies and other quiet areas.

Darker colors can be used to disguise problem areas such as uneven walls, or to make a high ceiling seem lower. In heavy-use areas, dark colors can help hide wear. Rough surfaces and flat paint finishes make colors seem darker because they absorb more light.

Dark walls tend to dominate, so you may choose to use lighter-colored accents to add balance to a room.

Dark colors absorb light to make a room seem quieter and more intimate. Dark colors work well in a library, den or study. Dark-colored walls in these rooms emphasize the light furnishings. Darker furnishings would blend into this type of room, creating a heavier atmosphere.

9

Warm Colors

Reds, yellows, browns, oranges and peaches are warm colors. Intense warm colors create exciting spaces, while subdued warm colors form pleasant rooms for social gatherings. Warm colors are often used in eating areas, like breakfast or dining rooms.

Warm colors also help make north rooms more inviting. Research has shown that people actually feel warmer in a room painted with yellows, reds or oranges than they do in a white or blue room. In colder climates, warm colors are a popular choice.

Warm colors range from intense yellows, reds and oranges to more subtle salmons and browns. Warm colors are common choices for morning rooms, or for active nighttime spaces. In colder climates, warm colors can make rooms seem cozy and more inviting.

Cool Colors

Blues, greens, lavenders and grays are cool colors. Intense cool colors are fresh and dramatic, while subdued cool grays are tranquil. Cool colors make rooms feel less confining. They are often used in bathrooms and other small rooms.

Use cool colors in west-facing kitchens, porches and other areas where afternoon heat is a problem. In very warm climates, using whites and cool colors exclusively can make an entire house seem more comfortable.

Cool colors range from bright violet, royal blue and jade green to pale mint green and rich indigo blue. Cool colors are frequently used in bedrooms and in formal living and dining areas. Bathrooms, dressing rooms and other small spaces feel less confining when decorated in cool colors.

Bright Colors

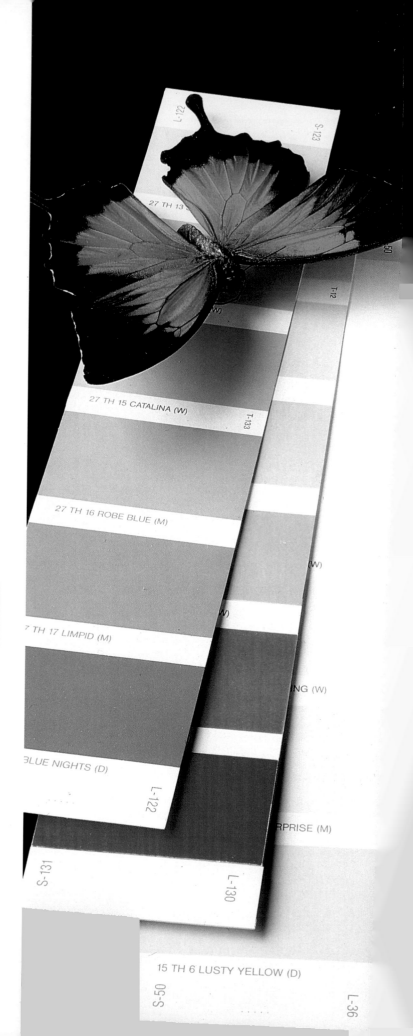

Bright colors are highly saturated with pigment. They are not diluted by white or darkened by black. Bright colors work well in active spaces like recreation rooms, sun porches and children's rooms.

Because bright colors draw attention, they are often used as accents in rooms with neutral or subdued color schemes.

Bright colors create excitement. They work well in active, informal spaces. Bright colors also work well in rooms with little natural light, such as basement recreation rooms.

12

26 TH 21 BEACHFRONT BLUE (W)

26 TH 22 BORN BLUE (M)

26 TH 23 BURNT BLUE (D)

26 TH 24 COAL BLUE

12 TH 2 WHITE

4 TH 3 TYRI

12 TH 3 PATINA (V

4 TH 4 MADO

12 TH 4 CRACKER (

4 TH 5 ROSE D

12 TH 5 LAMBSWOOL

4 TH 6 DUSK RED (D)

12 TH 6 SPANISH GOLD ON TILE (D)

Subdued Colors

Subdued colors are less saturated with pigment than bright colors. They are blended to include mixtures of white, black or gray. Subdued colors are relaxing and restful, and are frequently used in studies and bedrooms. Subdued colors form a soft background in bathrooms and dressing rooms.

You can increase visual interest in a subdued room by adding a few brightly colored accents.

Subdued colors are restful. Use them to create a tranquil mood in bedrooms and other quiet retreats.

Creating Moods with Color

Each color or combination of colors inspires a different feeling or mood. The color should appeal to the people who use the room. The combinations you may choose are limitless.

For an entryway or foyer, consider a bold color combination that makes a strong introduction to your home. For a guest bedroom, you might choose classic dark colors to create an elegant, formal feeling. In a teenager's bedroom, a surprising mixture of bright colors can be appropriate. In a master bedroom, you might be more comfortable with a restful combination of subdued colors.

In a library or study that is used by the whole family, you may use soft, related colors that create a tranquil mood. Natural tones like browns and beiges are a good choice for libraries and family rooms.

Bold color scheme in this room is created by the high contrast between whites and blacks, and between the complementary red and green. Hard-edged geometric patterns and dark walls contribute to the striking design.

Surprising color scheme uses several bright colors and fabrics. The unusual combination of fabric patterns adds to the dramatic effect.

Tranquil room is created by using cool related colors that have low contrast. The floral patterns repeated in the draperies, artwork and rug help unify the room.

Cheerful and airy mood is created by light colors that make the room seem larger. To maintain the open feeling, low-contrast pastel colors were chosen for the furnishings. The minimal window treatment opens the room to maximum sunlight.

Subtle, comfortable decorating scheme uses subdued complementary colors. The carefully placed pastel blues provide a cool contrast to the warm peach-colored walls.

Formal decorating scheme uses classically detailed patterns, rich fabrics and dark accent colors that draw attention. A darker wall would give this room a more intimate feeling.

Natural color scheme is created by using warm earth tones with simple patterns and textures. The sky blues in this room provide a cool accent to the natural warmth of the brown tones.

Geometric

Large print

Overall print

Small print

Pattern Basics

Wallcoverings increase visual interest by adding pattern, texture and accent color to a room. They are a dramatic way to quickly define a room style. For example, a bold abstract print immediately establishes a contemporary style, while a small floral design will suggest a more traditional or country theme.

Many vinyl wallcoverings are washable and are increasingly popular choices for kitchens, baths and high-traffic areas.

Your decorating center offers hundreds of different wallcovering designs that fall into four basic styles (shown at left): geometrics, large prints, overall prints and small prints. Many centers have decorating consultants who will help you with style and pattern selections at no charge.

Basic Wallcovering Patterns

Geometric patterns include plaids, stripes and grids. Large geometric patterns can be bold and exciting, while small patterns can be very subtle. Patterns with strong vertical lines make a ceiling seem higher.

Large prints add the most visual interest to a room. They can also make a room seem smaller and more intimate.

Overall prints form tight patterns. The eye blends the design together, minimizing pattern and emphasizing color. Overall prints can be used in any room.

Small prints add a touch of pattern to the overall background color, forming a subtle backdrop. They are often used in kitchens, bathrooms and other small spaces.

Textured wallcoverings

Texture paint

Coordinating wallcovering, border and fabric

Special Effects

Wallcoverings with coordinated fabrics, borders and textured surfaces expand your decorating options. Linen, grasscloth or textile wallcoverings will soften the appearance of a room. Embossed or expanded vinyl wallcoverings give walls three-dimensional texture. Texture paint is an inexpensive way to add interest or cover up an uneven surface.

Many manufacturers produce fabrics and borders that coordinate with wallcoverings. Wallcovering books contain samples of each, and may have photos showing how the elements can be combined. These photos offer a good source of ideas for wall treatments.

Sample books group coordinated wallcoverings, borders and fabrics. Sample books may have photos that show you how the elements can be combined.

Borders add interest. They can be used to blend coordinated wallcoverings, to frame windows, doors and ceilings, or as a chair rail on painted walls.

Coordinating fabrics and wallcoverings are available from manufacturers. Fabrics may match the wallcoverings or be complementary. The coordinates may also include matching or complementary borders.

Texture paint creates shadows and slight color differences for a more interesting wall surface. Working the wet paint with different tools produces a variety of texture effects.

Textured wallcoverings, like embossed or expanded vinyls, imitate the effect of plaster or texture paint on walls and ceilings. Textured wallcoverings have the added benefit of being easy to remove.

Creating Your Own Room Design

A successful decorating plan creatively blends the old with the new. Start by collecting samples from the furniture, carpeting or other elements you want to retain in the room.

Take a small sample of carpeting from an inconspicuous area, like a closet. Clip fabric swatches from hems and folds of upholstery and drapes. If possible, take samples of woodwork and tiles.

Next, visit decorating centers to collect samples of paint colors and wallcoverings. Clip out interesting ideas from magazines. As you assemble samples, spread them out in the room you intend to decorate. Try to imagine how new colors and patterns might look next to the existing furnishings. The best decorating scheme is one that pleases you and your family, so trust your own judgment when choosing colors and patterns.

Snip samples from inside drapery hems, and take samples of carpet threads from closet corners. Cut samples of upholstery fabrics from the undersides of furniture. Collect samples of flooring tiles and woodwork, if possible.

Clip ideas from decorating magazines, and collect paint, wallcovering and fabric samples during visits to home decorating centers.

Tape or staple samples to index cards. Use the cards to jot down measurements or to make small sketches and notes. Place samples in clear plastic bags so that you can see the contents easily. You will find this particularly useful if you are working on more than one room. Take your samples along to the decorating center as you begin making selections.

Building a Basic Color Scheme

Most room designs use one of three basic color schemes. A **single-color scheme** uses one color in varying shades, like light and dark blues. A **related color scheme** features colors that are next to each other on the color wheel. A room decorated in blues and lavenders is an example of a related color scheme. A **complementary color scheme** uses colors that are opposite each other on the color wheel, like peach and blue.

When redecorating a room, you can create a wide variety of color schemes even if the carpeting and furnishings remain the same.

Single-color Scheme

Use varying shades of the same color. A single-color scheme is easy to develop, and it lends a restful feeling to a room. You can tie two rooms together by using the same single-color scheme in both spaces. The choice of darker blues in this room allows the lighter furnishings to stand out.

Related Color Scheme

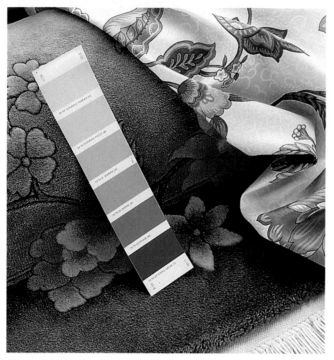 

Use colors that are close together on the color wheel. A related color scheme creates a unified, quiet room. Related light colors are relaxing, while related dark colors are elegant and formal.

Complementary Color Scheme

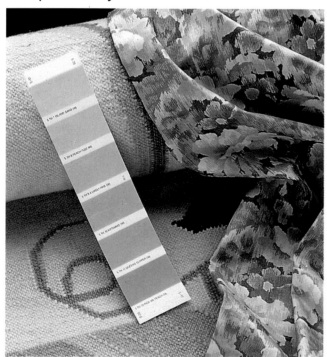 

Use colors found opposite each other on the color wheel. Complementary schemes are often dramatic. In this room, the warm peach is enhanced and balanced by cool blue accents. The lighter pastel walls allow the light-colored furnishings to blend into the room.

Selecting Paint & Wallcovering

When you begin shopping for a new paint color or wallcovering, bring fabric swatches and other samples of your home furnishings to the decorating center.

Many decorating centers have professional design consultants who help customers at no charge. The paint selection display in a home decorating center can hold more than a thousand different colors, and wallcovering departments may have several hundred sample books. By comparing the samples from your home with the store's paint swatches and wallcovering samples, you can narrow your selections quickly.

Always bring several paint or wallcovering samples back to your home for a day or two before making a final selection. Look at the samples in the room you are decorating to see how the colors and patterns interact with the existing furnishings. Remember that colors change under different lighting conditions, so look at your samples in bright daylight, on a cloudy day and under artificial light.

23

Tips for Selecting Paint & Wallcovering

In the store, check paint chips and wallcovering samples in daylight as well as under artificial lighting. Store lighting can differ from home lighting.

Take home no more than 3 different color and wallcovering samples. Fewer alternatives make the final decision easier.

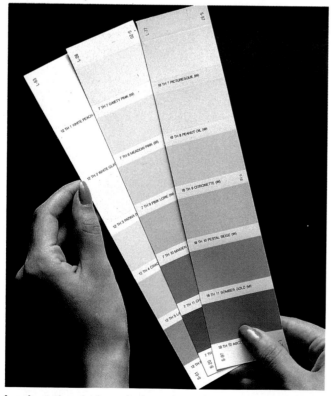

Look at the dark end of a paint chip card to determine the tint base of an off-white paint. Almost all off-whites have a hint of color.

Choose wallcovering books by flipping quickly through them. A quick glance saves time and can tell you which books you will want to study more carefully.

Tape 4 paint chips together. Larger color samples are easier to judge. Cut off white borders, which can be distracting.

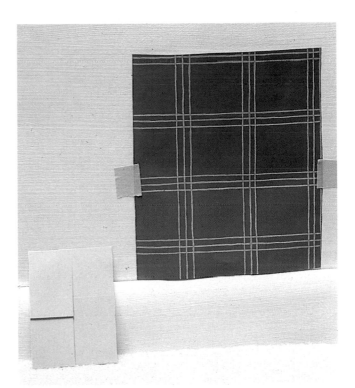

Judge samples of paint and wallcovering in the room where they will be used. Stand color samples upright to duplicate the way light strikes a wall surface. Tape wallcovering samples against the walls where they will be hung.

Before making final decision, cut a large sample of wallcovering to use in the 24-hour test. Decorating centers will usually give large samples, or may let you borrow sample books.

Buy a quart of your chosen paint color. Paint a large sample card to hang on the wall. Follow the 24-hour test before buying the full amounts of paint and wall-covering needed.

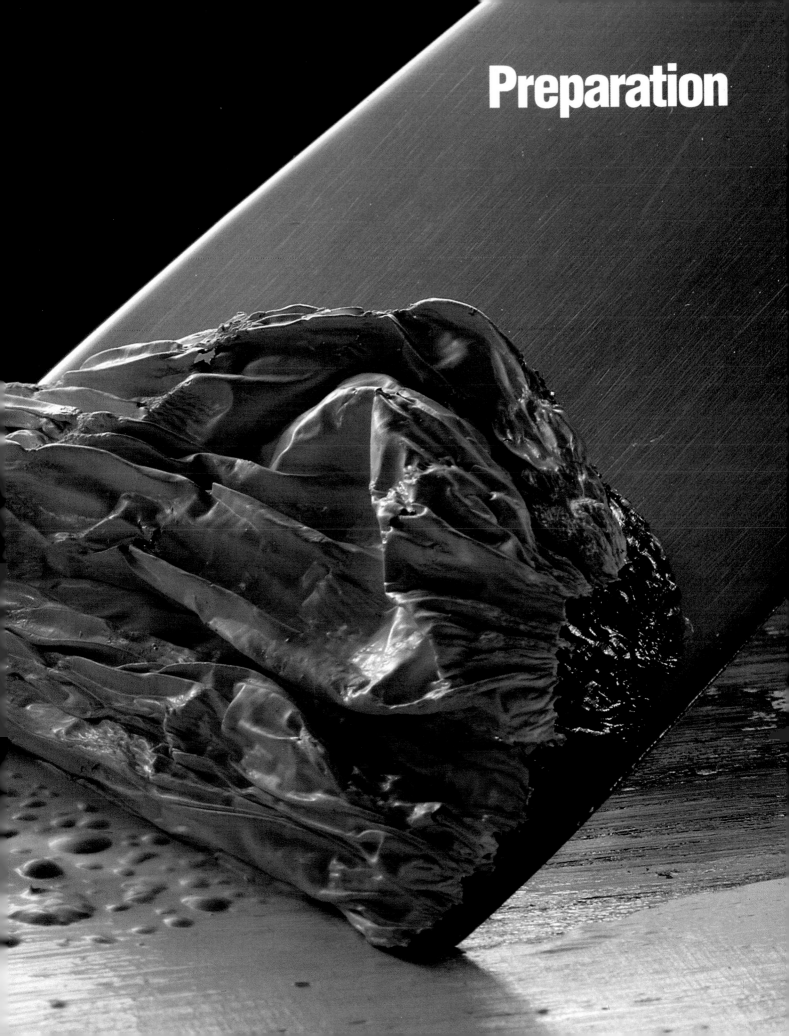

Preparation

Ladders & Scaffolds

Two quality stepladders and an extension plank are all you need to paint most interior surfaces. For painting high areas, build a simple scaffold by running the plank through the steps of two stepladders. It is easy to lose your balance or step off the plank, so choose tall ladders for safety. The upper part of the ladders can help you balance, and will keep you from stepping off the ends of the plank. Buy a strong, straight 2 × 10-inch plank no more than 12 feet long, or rent a plank from a material dealer or rental outlet.

Manufacturer's sticker gives weight ratings and instructions for correct use of the ladder. Read it carefully when shopping for a ladder. Remember that you may exceed its recommended weight limits when you carry tools or materials up a ladder.

How to Use a Scaffold

For ceilings and high spots on walls, make a simple scaffold by running an extension plank through the steps of 2 stepladders. Plank should be no more than 12 feet long. Ladders should face away from one another, so that steps are to inside. Make sure the ladder braces are down and locked, and watch your footing.

How to Use a Scaffold on Stairways

For stairs run an extension plank through the step of a ladder, and place the other end on a stairway step. Make sure the ladder is steady, and check to see that the plank is level. Keep the plank close to the wall, if possible, and never overreach.

Rent extension planks from a paint dealer or from a rental center.

Choose straight planks without large knots or splinters. Choose 2 × 10" boards that have some spring in them: stiff, brittle wooden planks can break unexpectedly.

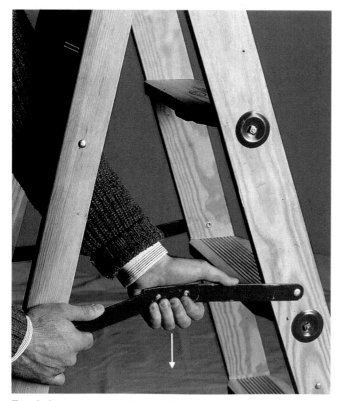

Push braces completely down and make certain they are locked. Legs of the ladder should be level and steady against the ground.

Do not stand on top step, top brace or on the utility shelf of a stepladder.

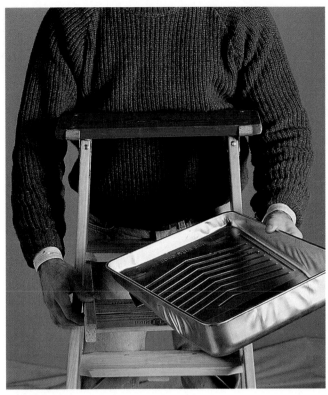

Center your weight on the ladder. Move the ladder often; don't overreach.

Keep steps tight by periodically checking them and tightening the braces when they need it.

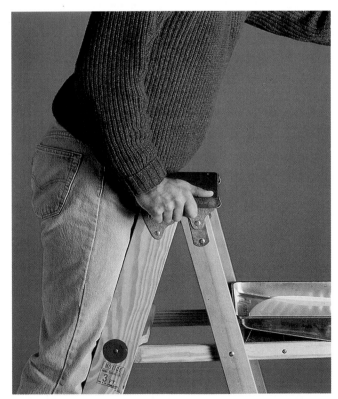

Keep ladder in front of you when working. Lean your body against the ladder for balance.

Adjustable ladder adapts to many different work needs. It can be used as a straight ladder, a stepladder or as a base for scaffold planks.

Work light

Bucket &
natural
sponge

Drop
cloth

Sprayer

Rubber
gloves

Palm
sander

Wet
sander

Heat
gun

Wallboard
knives

Hand
vacuum

Screw gun

Perforation tool

Paint brush

Tools & Materials for Preparation

You can reduce or eliminate most cleanup chores by buying the right prep tools. For example, buy plastic or paper throwaway pails for mixing patching plaster, taping compound or spackle. When the patcher hardens in the container, just throw it away: you'll avoid the job of washing out the pail and also avoid plugging plumbing drains with plaster.

Use a sponge or wallboard wet sander to smooth plaster or wallboard compound while it is still soft,

rather than waiting until it dries and becomes hard to sand.

Buy a variety of patching tools. You will need narrow putty knives for reaching into small spaces, and a wider knife or trowel that just spans the repair area when patching holes in walls or ceilings. A patching tool that overlaps both edges of the hole will let you patch with one pass of the tool, reducing trowel marks and eliminating sanding.

Removal agents help prepare surfaces for paint and wallcovering, and speed cleanup. Clockwise from top left: wallpaper dough, cleanup solution, wallcovering remover, trisodium phosphate (TSP).

Preparation liquids, clockwise from top left: paint remover, liquid deglosser for dulling glossy surfaces prior to painting, latex bonding agent for plaster repairs.

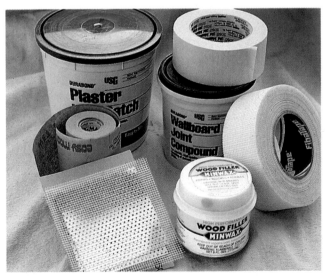

Patching and masking products, clockwise from top left: patching plaster, masking tape, premixed wallboard compound, fiberglass wallboard tape, wood patch, peel-and-stick metal patch, pre-gummed masking paper.

Primer & sealers provide a good base coat that bonds with paint or varnish finish. From left: sanding sealer, PVA primer, shellac, alkyd wallboard primer.

Removing Wallcovering

Newer vinyl wallcoverings can often be peeled off by hand. Some will leave a paper and adhesive residue that is easily removed with water. With non-peelable wallcoverings, pierce the surface with a perforation tool, then apply remover solution to dissolve the adhesive.

Wallcovering remover fluids contain wetting agents that penetrate the paper and help soften the adhesive. Use a remover solution to wash away old adhesive after wallcovering is removed.

If the old wallcovering was hung over unsealed wallboard, it may be impossible to remove it without destroying the wallboard. You may be able to paint or hang new wallcovering directly over the old wallcovering, but the surface should be smooth and primed. Before painting over wallcovering, prime with alkyd wallboard primer.

1 Find a loose edge and try to strip wallcovering. Vinyls often peel away easily.

2 If wallcovering does not strip by hand, cover floor with layers of newspaper. Add wallcovering remover fluid to bucket of water, as directed by manufacturer.

3 Pierce the surface of wallcovering with perforation tool. This allows the remover solution to enter and soften the adhesive.

4 Use a sprayer, paint roller or sponge to apply remover solution. Let moisture soak into covering, according to manufacturer's directions.

5 Peel away loosened wallcovering with a 6-inch broadknife. Be careful not to damage the plaster or wallboard. Remove all backing paper.

6 Rinse adhesive residue from wall with remover solution. Rinse with clear water and let walls dry completely.

Preparing & Repairing Walls & Ceilings

Thoroughly washing, rinsing and sanding your walls before priming will guarantee a long-lasting finish. For a professional appearance, carefully check your walls for damage and repair the wallboard or plaster as needed. Pregummed fiberglass repair tapes and premixed patching compounds reduce drying time and let you patch and paint a wall the same day.

Wash and sand before repainting. Use TSP (trisodium phosphate) solution and a sponge to cut grease and to remove dirt. Wear rubber gloves, and wash walls from the bottom up with a damp sponge to avoid streaks. Rinse thoroughly with clean water. After drying, sand surfaces lightly.

How to Remove Stains

1 Apply stain remover to a clean, dry cloth, and rub lightly to remove the stain.

2 Seal all stain areas with white pigmented shellac. Pigmented shellac prevents stains from bleeding through the new paint. **Do not use clear shellac as shown in photo.**

Water or rust stains may indicate water damage. Check for leaking pipes and soft plaster, make needed repairs, then seal area with stain-killing sealer.

How to Remove Mildew

1 Test stains by washing with water and detergent. Mildew stains will not wash out.

2 Wearing rubber gloves and eye protection, wash the walls with bleach, which kills mildew spores.

3 After bleach treatment, wash mildew away with TSP solution, and rinse with clear water.

How to Patch Peeling Paint

1 Scrape away loose paint with a putty knife or paint scraper.

2 Apply spackle to the edges of chipped paint with a putty knife or flexible wallboard knife.

3 Sand the patch area with 150-grit production sandpaper. Patch area should feel smooth to the touch.

How to Fill Nail Holes

1 Apply lightweight spackle to the hole with a putty knife or your fingertip. This keeps repair area small so it is easy to hide with paint. Let spackle dry.

2 Sand the repair area lightly with 150-grit production sandpaper. Production paper has an open surface that does not clog. Wipe dust away with a damp sponge, then prime the spot with PVA primer.

How to Fill Shallow Dents & Holes

1 Scrape or sand away any loose plaster, peeled paint or wallboard face paper to ensure a solid base for patching.

2 Fill hole with lightweight spackle. Apply spackle with smallest wallboard knife that will span the entire hole. Let spackle dry.

3 Sand lightly with 150-grit production sandpaper.

How to Fix Popped Wallboard Nails

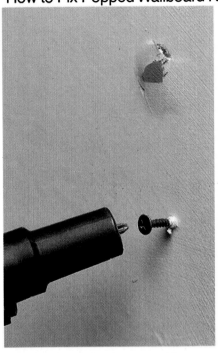  

1 Drive wallboard screw 2" away from popped nail. Be sure the screw hits the stud or joist and pulls the wallboard tight against the framing.

2 Scrape away loose paint or wallboard compound. Drive the popped nail back into the framing so the head is sunk 1/32" below the surface of the wallboard. Do not set the nail with a punch.

3 Apply a second thin coat if necessary to conceal the tape edges. Sand lightly and prime the repair area. Retexture the surface.

How to Repair Cracks in Plaster

1 Scrape away any texture or loose plaster around the crack. Reinforce crack with pregummed fiberglass wallboard tape.

2 Use taping knife or trowel to apply spackle or wallboard compound over tape so that tape is just concealed: if compound is too thick, it will recrack.

3 Apply a second thin coat if necessary to conceal the tape edges. Sand lightly and prime the repair area. Retexture the surface (pages 84-85).

Preparing Woodwork

Before painting, woodwork should be cleaned, patched, and sanded. Make certain that all peeling or loose paint is scraped away before doing any patching. If the old paint is heavily layered or badly chipped, it should be stripped before the wood is patched and repainted. If new hardware is to be installed, check to see if new pieces will fit old screw holes. If new holes must be drilled, fill the old holes with wood patch.

If using a heat gun to strip wood, take care not to scorch the wood. Never use a heat gun after using chemical strippers: the chemical residue may be vaporized or ignited by the heat.

When using a chemical paint stripper, always wear protective clothing and safety gear, including eye protection and a respirator. Follow the label directions for safe use, and always work in a well-ventilated area.

1 Follow label directions for safe use of chemicals. Wear heavy rubber gloves and eye protection, use drop cloths, and open windows and doors for ventilation when using chemical strippers.

2 Apply a liberal coat of stripper to painted wood with a paint brush or steel wool. Let it stand until paint begins to blister. Do not let stripper dry out on wood surfaces.

3 Scrape away paint with a putty knife or scraper and steel wool as soon as it softens. Rub stripped wood with denatured alcohol and new steel wool to help clean grain. Wipe wood with a wet sponge or solvent, as directed on stripper label.

How to Remove Paint with a Heat Gun

1 Hold heat gun near wood until paint softens and just begins to blister. Overheating can make the paint gummy, and may scorch the wood. Always be careful when using a heat gun around flammable materials.

2 Remove softened paint with a scraper or putty knife. Scrapers are available in many shapes for removing paint from shaped moldings. Sand away any paint residue remaining after heat stripping.

How to Prepare Woodwork for Painting

1 Scrape away any peeling or loose paint. Badly chipped woodwork should be stripped. Use a putty knife to apply latex wood patch or spackle to any nail holes, dents, and to any other damaged areas.

2 Sand surfaces with 150-grit production paper until they are smooth to the touch. Wipe woodwork with a tack cloth before priming and painting.

41

Masking & Draping

For fast, mess-free painting, shield any surfaces that could get splattered. If painting only the ceiling, drape the walls and woodwork to prevent splatters. When painting walls, mask the baseboards and the window and door casings.

Remove lightweight furniture, and move heavier pieces to the center of the room and cover with plastic. Cover the floors with 9-ounce canvas drop cloths that will absorb paint splatters.

Masking & draping materials, clockwise from top left: plastic and canvas drop cloths, self-adhesive plastic, masking tape, pregummed masking papers. Plastic-paper laminates are also available.

How to Drape Walls

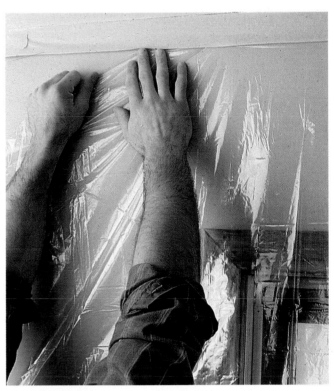

1 Press top half of 2" masking tape along ceiling-wall corners. Leave bottom half of tape loose.

2 Hang sheet plastic under masking tape, draping walls and baseboards. Remove loose edge as soon as the paint is too dry to run.

How to Mask Wood Trim

1 Use pregummed paper or wide masking tape to protect wood moldings from paint splatters. Leave outside edge of masking tape loose.

2 After applying tape, run the tip of a putty knife along inside edge of tape to seal against seeping paint. Remove masking material as soon as paint is too dry to run.

Final Check & Cleanup Tips

Before painting, make a final check of the work area. Clean the room thoroughly to eliminate dust that might collect on tools and settle on wet paint. Maintain the temperature and humidity levels recommended by product labels. This will help keep paint edges wet while painting, to avoid lap marks in the finished job.

It is also important for the paint to dry within normal time limits so dirt can't settle on the finish while it is wet. When applying wallcovering, a proper work climate prevents premature drying of the adhesive, and blisters or loose edges on the wallcovering.

Check all surfaces to be painted with a strong side-light. Sand, or spackle and sand, any rough spots that were missed in preparation.

Turn off thermostats for forced air furnaces and air-conditioners so that the fan will not circulate dust through the area being painted.

Sand all surfaces that will be painted with 150-grit production sandpaper. Sanding dulls the surface so it will accept new paint. Wipe walls with tack rag.

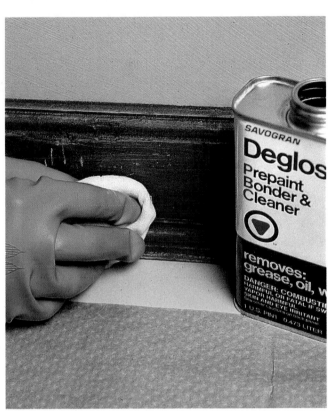

Wipe dust from woodwork with a tack rag, or with a clean cloth and liquid deglosser.

Use a vacuum cleaner to pick up the dust from windowsills and window tracks, and from baseboards and casements.

If humidity levels are low, place a humidifier in the room before painting or wallcovering. This keeps paint or adhesive from drying too fast.

Applying Primers & Sealers

A sealer should be applied to wood surfaces before they are varnished. Wood often has both hard and soft grains, as well as a highly absorbent end grain. Applying a sealer helps close the wood surface so that varnish is absorbed evenly in different types of wood grain. If the wood is not sealed, the varnish may dry to a mottled finish.

Primers are used to seal surfaces that will be painted. Wallboard seams and patch areas that have been treated with wallboard compound or patching material can absorb paint at a different rate than the surrounding areas. Joints and patch areas often show or "shadow" through the finished paint if the walls were not adequately primed.

Tint primer with color base available at paint dealers, or request that your dealer tint the primer. A color-matched primer provides an excellent base for finish coat paints.

How to Prime & Seal Before Painting

Seal raw wood by applying a primer before painting or a clear sealer before varnishing. Unsealed wood can produce a spotty finish.

Roughen gloss surfaces with fine sandpaper, then prime to provide good bonding between the new and the old paint. Primers provide "tooth" for the new coat of paint.

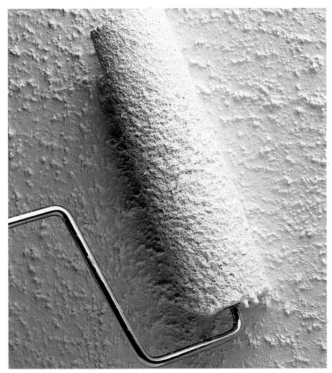

Seal textured surfaces with a PVA or alkyd primer, then apply finish coat with a long-nap roller. Textured walls and ceilings soak up a lot of paint and make it difficult to apply paint evenly.

Spot-prime minor repair areas on plaster or wallboard with PVA primer.

Painting

Painting Safety

Always read and follow the label information on paint and solvent containers. Chemicals that pose a fire hazard are listed (in order of flammability) as: combustible, flammable, or extremely flammable. Use caution when using these products, and remember that the fumes are also flammable.

The warning "use with adequate ventilation" means that there should be no more vapor buildup than there would be if using the material outside. Open doors and windows, use exhaust fans and an approved safety mask if you can smell paint or solvent.

Paint chemicals do not store well. Buy just as much as is needed for the project and keep chemicals away from children. Use up excess paint by applying an extra coat or follow local guidelines regarding paint disposal.

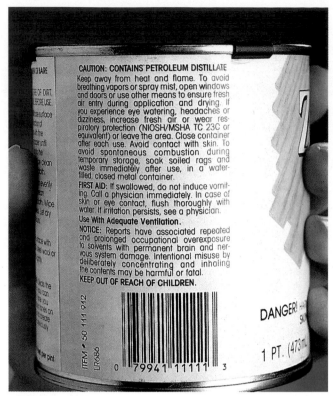

Read label information. Chemicals that are poisonous or flammable are labeled with warnings and instructions for safe handling.

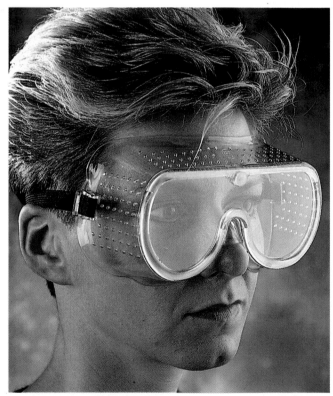

Wear safety goggles when using chemical stripper or cleaning products. Use goggles when painting overhead.

Do not use chemicals that are listed as combustible or flammable, such as paint strippers, near an open flame. Appliance pilot lights can ignite chemical vapors.

Open windows and doors and use a fan for ventilation when painting indoors. If a product label has the warning "harmful or fatal if swallowed," assume that the vapors are dangerous to breathe.

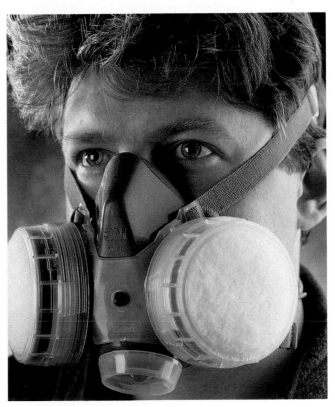

Use an approved mask to filter vapors if you cannot ventilate a work area properly. If you can smell vapors, the ventilation is not adequate.

Let thinners stand after cleaning tools. After the solid material settles out, pour off the clear thinner and save for reuse. Discard sediment.

Dispose of leftover paint safely. Let container stand uncovered until solvent evaporates, then re-cover and dispose of the container with other trash.

Choosing Paint

Paints are either water-base latex or alkyd-base. **Latex paint** is easy to apply and clean up, and the improved chemistry of today's latexes makes them suitable for nearly every application. Some painters feel that **alkyd paint** allows for a smoother finished surface, but local regulations may restrict the use of alkyd-base products.

Paints come in various sheens. Paint finishes range from flat to high-gloss enamels. Gloss enamels dry to a shiny finish, and are used for surfaces that will be washed often, like bathrooms, kitchens and woodwork. Flat paints are used for most wall and ceiling applications.

Always use a good primer to coat surfaces before painting. The primer bonds well to all surfaces, and provides a durable base that keeps the finish coat from cracking or peeling. Tint the primer to match the new color to avoid the need for a second coat of expensive finish paint.

How to Estimate Paint

1) Length of wall or ceiling (feet)	
2) Height of wall, or width of ceiling	×
3) Surface area	=
4) Coverage per gallon of chosen paint	÷
5) **Gallons of paint needed**	=

How to Select a Quality Paint

Paint coverage listed on label of quality paint should be about 400 square feet per gallon. Bargain paints (left) may require 2 or even 3 coats to cover the same area.

High washability is a feature of quality paint. The pigments in bargain paints (right) may "chalk" and wash away with mild scrubbing.

Paint Sheens

Range of sheens, from left: **Gloss enamel,** a highly reflective finish for areas where high washability is important. All gloss paints tend to show surface flaws. Alkyd-base enamels have highest gloss. **Medium-gloss** latex enamel, a highly washable surface with a slightly less reflective finish. Like gloss enamels, medium-gloss paints tend to show surface flaws. **Eggshell enamel,** combining soft finish with the washability of enamel. **Flat latex,** an all-purpose paint with a soft finish that hides surface irregularities.

Work light

60W

³⁄₈'' nap roller

Paint tray

3'' paintbrush

2'' trim brush

Tapered sash brush

Painting Tools & Equipment

Most painting jobs can be done with a few quality tools. Purchase two or three premium brushes, a sturdy paint pan that can be attached to a step-ladder, and one or two good rollers. With proper cleanup, these tools will last for years.

Brushes made of hog or ox bristles should be used only with alkyd-base paints. All-purpose brushes blend polyester, nylon, and sometimes animal bristles. Choose a straight-edged 3" wall brush, a 2" straight-edged trim brush, and a tapered sash brush.

How to Choose a Paintbrush

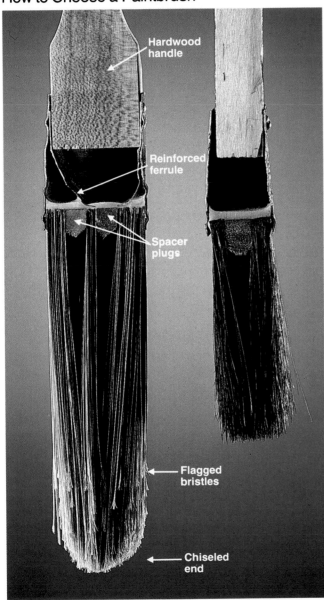

Quality brush, shown in left cutaway, has shaped hardwood handle and a sturdy reinforced ferrule made of noncorrosive metal. Multiple spacer plugs separate bristles. Quality brush has flagged (split) bristles and a chiseled end for precise edging. A cheaper brush will have a blunt end, unflagged bristles and a cardboard spacer plug that may soften when wet.

3" straight-edged brush (top) is a good choice for cutting paint lines at ceilings and in corners. For painting woodwork, a 2" trim brush (middle) works well. Choose brushes with chiseled tips for painting in corners. A tapered sash brush (bottom) may help when painting corners on window sashes.

Choosing Rollers & Roller Accessories

A good paint roller is an inexpensive, timesaving tool that can last for years. Choose a standard 9-inch roller with a wire frame and nylon bearings. The roller should feel well balanced, and should have a handle molded to fit your hand. The handle should also have a threaded end that lets you attach an extension for painting ceilings and high walls.

Roller covers are available in a wide variety of nap lengths, but most jobs can be done with ⅜" nap. Select medium-priced **synthetic** roller covers that can be reused a few times before discarding. Bargain roller covers might shed fibers onto the painted surface, and cannot be cleaned and reused. Rinse all roller covers in solvent to prevent lint.

Use more expensive **lamb's wool** roller covers when using most alkyd-base paints. **Mohair** covers work well with gloss alkyd paints where complete smoothness is important.

Nap length. Select proper roller cover for the surface you intend to paint. ¼"-nap covers (top) are used for very flat surfaces. ⅜"-nap covers (middle) will cover the small flaws found in most flat walls and ceilings. 1"-nap covers (bottom) fill spaces in rough surfaces, like concrete blocks or stucco walls.

Cover material. Synthetic covers (left) are good with most paints, especially latexes. Wool or mohair roller covers (right) give an even finish with alkyd products. Choose better quality roller covers that do not shed lint.

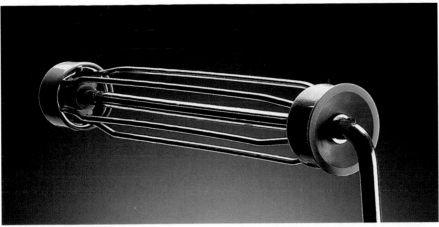

Choose sturdy roller handle with wire cage construction. Nylon bearings should roll smoothly and easily when you spin the cage. The handle end should be threaded for attaching an extension handle.

Buy paint tray with legs that allow the tray to sit steadily on the shelf of a stepladder. A good paint tray will resist flexing when it is twisted. Look for a textured ramp that keeps the roller turning easily.

Five-gallon paint container and paint screen speeds painting of large areas. Load paint roller straight from bucket, using a roller extension handle. Do not try to balance pail on stepladder shelf.

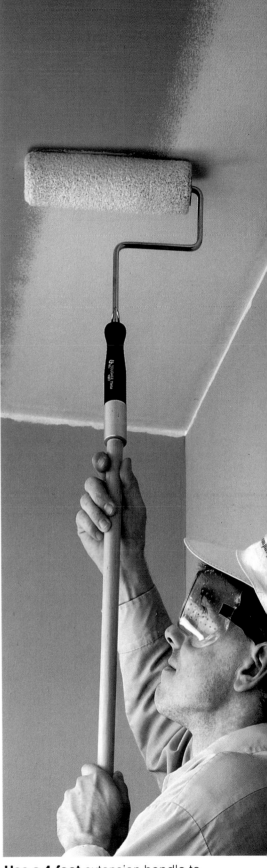

Use a 4-foot extension handle to paint ceilings and walls easily without a ladder.

Special Painting Tools

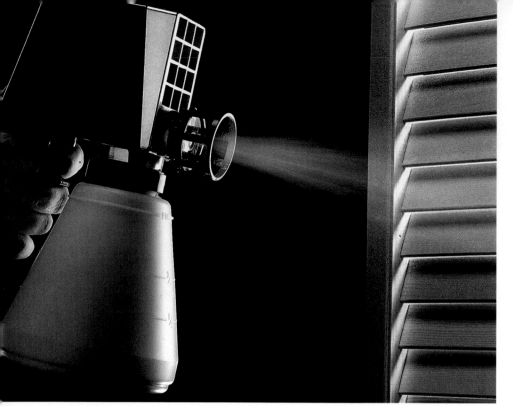

Airless paint sprayer is useful for painting large areas, or for irregular surfaces like louvered closet doors or heat registers. All sprayers produce some overspray, so wear protective gear and mask off all areas likely to be splattered. Movable workpieces should be painted outside or in your basement or garage. Thinning the paint before spraying will result in easier use of the tool and more even coverage.

Surfaces with unusual angles and contours are sometimes difficult to paint with standard rollers and brushes. Specialty tools make some painting situations easier. Disposable foam brushes, for instance, are excellent for applying an even coat of clear varnish to smooth woodwork.

Specialty rollers & pads come in various shapes for painting edges, corners, and other unique applications.

Bendable tool can be shaped to fit unusual surfaces, such as window shutters or the fins of cast-iron radiators.

Paint glove simplifies painting of pipes and other contoured surfaces, like wrought-iron.

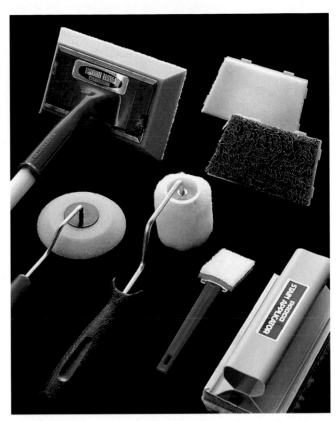

Paint pads and specialty rollers come in a wide range of sizes and shapes to fit different painting needs.

Aerosol spray paint speeds painting of any small, intricate job, like painting heat registers.

Paint mixer bit attaches to power drill to stir paints quickly and easily. Use variable-speed drill at low speed to avoid air bubbles in paint.

Mix paint together (called "boxing") in a large pail to eliminate slight color variations between cans. Stir the paint thoroughly with a wooden stick or power drill attachment. Keep paint from building up in the groove around the paint can lid. Pound several small nail holes into the groove to let paint drip back into the can.

Basic Painting Techniques

For a professional-looking paint job, paint must be spread evenly onto the work surfaces without running, dripping or lapping onto other areas. Excess paint will run on the surface and can drip onto woodwork and floors. Stretching paint too far leaves lap marks and causes incomplete coverage.

Painting with brushes and rollers is a three-step process. Paint is first applied, is next distributed evenly, and is finally smoothed out for an even finish.

How to Use a Paint Brush

1 Dip the brush, loading one-third of bristle length. Tap the bristles against the side of the can. Dipping deeper overloads the brush. Dragging the brush against the lip of the can causes the bristles to wear.

2 Cut in edges using narrow edge of brush, pressing just enough to flex the bristles. Keep an eye on the paint edge, and paint with long slow strokes. Always paint from dry area back into wet paint to avoid lap marks.

3 Brush wall corners using wide edge of brush. Paint open areas with brush or roller before brushed paint dries.

4 To paint large areas with a brush, apply paint with 2 or 3 diagonal strokes. Hold brush at about 45° angle to work surface, pressing just enough to flex bristles. Distribute paint evenly with horizontal strokes.

5 Smooth off surface by drawing brush vertically from top to bottom of painted area. Use light strokes and lift the brush from the surface at end of each stroke. This method is best for slow-drying alkyd enamels.

Using a Paint Roller

Paint surfaces in small sections, working from dry surfaces back into wet paint to avoid roller marks. If a paint job takes more than a day, cover the roller tightly with plastic wrap or store it in a bucket of water overnight to prevent paint from drying out.

1 Wet the roller cover with water (when painting with latex paint) or mineral spirits (when painting with alkyd enamel), to remove lint and prime the roller cover. Squeeze out excess solvent. Fill the paint tray reservoir. Dip roller fully into reservoir to load paint.

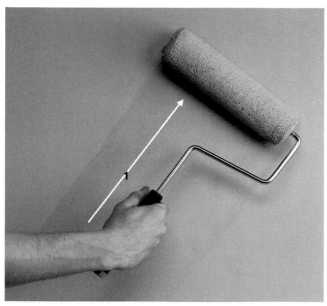

3 With the loaded roller, make a diagonal sweep (1) about 4' long on surface. On walls, roll upward on the first stroke to avoid spilling paint. Use slow roller strokes to avoid splattering.

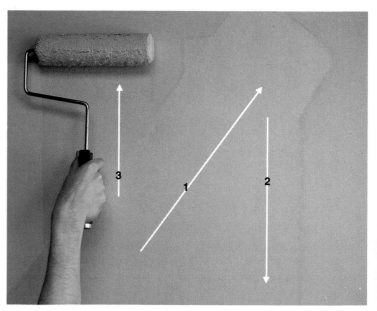

4 Draw roller straight down (2) from top of diagonal sweep. Move roller to beginning of diagonal and roll up (3) to complete unloading of roller.

2 Lift the roller from the paint reservoir, and roll back-and-forth on the textured ramp to distribute the paint evenly on the nap. Roller should be full but not dripping when lifted from the paint pan.

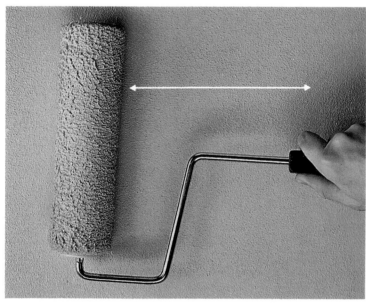

5 Distribute paint over section with horizontal back-and-forth strokes.

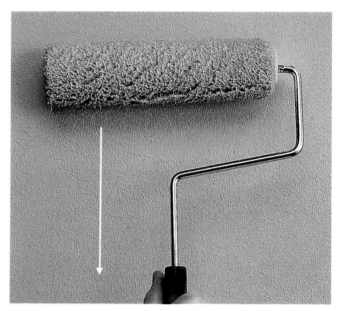

6 Smooth off area by lightly drawing roller vertically from top to bottom of painted area. Lift roller and return it to top of area after each stroke.

Painting Trim

When painting an entire room, paint the wood trim first, then the walls. Start by painting the inside portions of trim and working out toward walls. On windows, for instance, first paint the edges close to the glass, then the surrounding face trim.

Doors should be painted quickly because of the large surface. To avoid lap marks, always paint from dry surfaces back into wet paint. On baseboards, cut in the top edge and work down to the flooring. Plastic floor guards or a wide broadknife can help shield carpet and wood flooring from paint drips.

Alkyds and latex enamels may require two coats. Always sand lightly between coats and wipe with a tack cloth so that the second coat bonds properly.

How to Paint a Window

1 To paint double-hung windows, remove them from frames, if possible. Newer, spring-mounted windows are released by pushing against the frame (arrow).

2 Drill holes and insert 2 nails into the legs of wooden stepladder, and mount the window easel-style for easy painting; or lay window flat on bench or sawhorses. Do not paint sides or bottom of sashes.

3 Using a tapered sash brush, begin by painting the wood next to the glass. Use narrow edge of brush, and overlap paint onto the glass to create a weatherseal.

4 Clean excess paint off glass with a putty knife wrapped in a clean cloth. Rewrap the knife often so that you always wipe with clean fabric. Leave 1/16' paint overlap from sash onto glass.

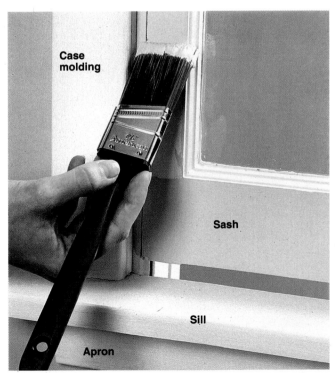

Case molding

Sash

Sill

Apron

5 Paint flat portions of sashes (1), then the case moldings (2), sill (3) and apron (4). Use slow brush strokes, and avoid getting paint between sash and frame.

6 If you must paint windows in place, move the painted windows up and down several times during the drying period to keep them from sticking. Use putty knife to avoid touching painted surface.

How to Paint Doors

1 Remove the door by driving lower hinge pin out with a screwdriver and hammer. Have a helper hold door in place. Drive out the upper hinge pin.

2 Place the door flat on sawhorses to paint. On paneled doors, paint in the following order: 1) recessed panels, 2) horizontal rails, and 3) vertical stiles.

3 Let door dry. If a second coat of paint is needed, sand lightly and wipe the door with tack cloth before repainting.

4 Seal the unpainted edges of the door with clear wood sealer to prevent moisture from entering wood. Water can cause wood to warp and swell.

Tips for Painting Trim

Protect wall and floor surfaces with a wide broadknife, or with plastic shielding tool.

Wipe paint off of broadknife or shielding tool each time it is moved.

Paint both sides of cabinet doors. This provides an even moisture seal and prevents warping.

Paint deep patterned surfaces with a stiff-bristled brush, like this stenciling brush. Use small circular strokes to penetrate recesses.

Painting Ceilings & Walls

For a smooth finish on large wall and ceiling areas, paint in small sections. First use a paintbrush to cut in the edge, then immediately roll the section before moving on. If brushed edges are left to dry before the large surfaces are rolled, visible lap marks will be left on the finished wall. Working in natural light makes it easier to spot missed areas.

Choose quality paint and tools, and work with a full brush or roller to avoid lap marks and assure full coverage. Keep roller speed slow to minimize paint splattering.

Tips for Painting Ceilings & Walls

Paint to a wet edge. Cut in edge on small section with a paintbrush just before rolling, then move on to next section. With two painters, let one cut in with a brush while the other rolls large areas.

Minimize brush marks. Slide roller cover slightly off when rolling near ceiling line or wall corners. Brushed areas dry to a different finish than rolled paint.

How to Paint Ceilings

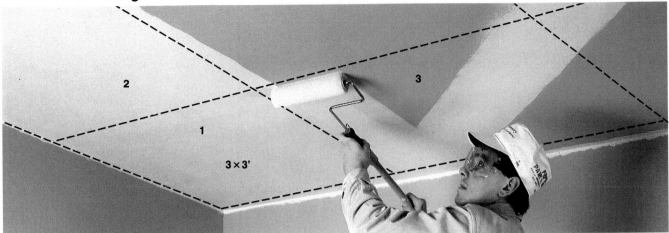

Paint ceilings with a roller handle extension. Use eye protection while painting overhead. Start at the corner farthest from the entry door. Paint the ceiling along the narrow end in 3 × 3' sections, cutting in the edges with a brush before rolling. Apply paint with diagonal stroke. Distribute paint evenly with back-and-forth strokes. For the final smoothing strokes, roll each section toward the entry wall, lifting the roller at the end of each sweep.

How to Paint Walls

Paint walls in 2 × 4' sections. Start in an upper corner, cutting in ceiling and wall corners with a brush, then rolling the section. Make initial diagonal stroke of roller from bottom of section upward, to avoid dripping paint. Distribute paint evenly with horizontal strokes, then finish with downward sweeps of the roller. Next, cut in and roll the section directly underneath. Continue with adjacent areas, cutting in and rolling top sections before bottom. All finish strokes should be rolled toward the floor.

Cleaning Up

At the end of a paint job you may choose to throw away the roller covers, but the paint pans, roller handles and brushes can be cleaned and stored for future use. Stray paint drips can be wiped away if they are still wet. A putty knife or razor will remove many dried paint spots on hardwood or glass. Remove stubborn paint from most surfaces with a chemical cleaner.

Use spinner tool to remove paint and solvent. Wash the roller cover or brush with solvent, then attach to the spinner. Pumping the handle throws liquids out of the roller cover or brush. Hold the spinner inside a cardboard box or 5-gallon pail to catch paint and avoid splatters.

Cleaning products, from left: chemical cleaner, spinner tool, cleaner tool for brushes and roller covers.

Cleanup Tips

Comb brush bristles with spiked side of cleaner tool. This aligns the bristles so they dry properly.

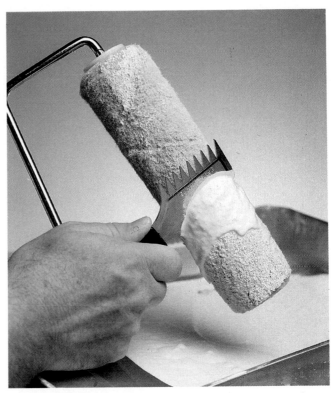

Scrape paint from roller cover with curved side of cleaner tool. Remove as much paint as possible before washing tools with solvent.

Store brushes in their original wrappers, or fold the bristles inside brown wrapping paper. Store washed roller covers on end to avoid flattening the nap.

Remove dried splatters with a chemical cleaner. Before using cleaner, test an inconspicuous area to make sure surface is colorfast.

Wallcovering

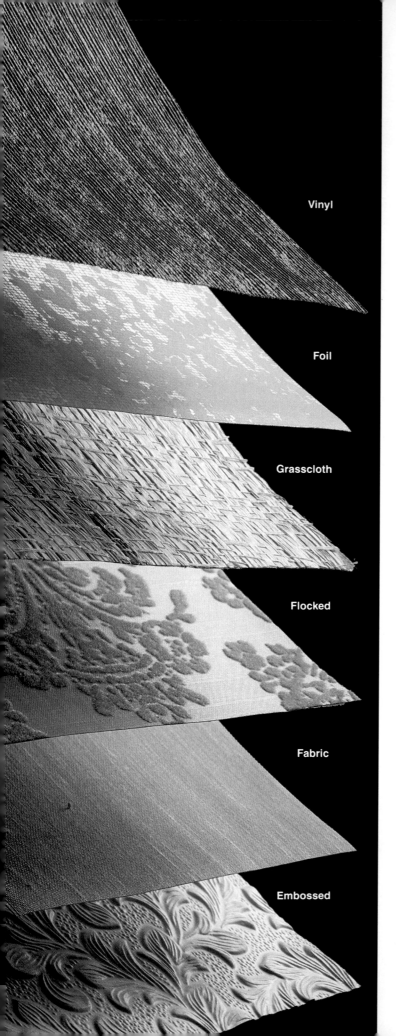

Vinyl

Foil

Grasscloth

Flocked

Fabric

Embossed

Choosing the Right Wallcovering

Very few modern "wallpapers" are actually made of paper. Today's wallcoverings may be made of vinyl, vinyl-coated paper or cloth, textiles, natural grasses, foil or mylar. Vinyl or coated vinyl coverings are the easiest to hang, clean and remove. Other types of wallcoverings can give a room a unique look, but may require special handling. Your choice of wallcovering depends on the needs of the room and on your confidence and ability.

Types of Wallcovering

Vinyl wallcoverings are made with a continuous flexible film, often applied over a fabric or paper backing. Some vinyls successfully duplicate the effect of natural grasscloth or textile wallcoverings. Because they are easy to apply, clean and remove, vinyl wallcoverings with preapplied adhesives are a good choice.

Foils or mylars are coated with a thin, flexible metallic film. These highly reflective wallcoverings add brightness to any room, but they require careful handling. Foils also reveal all wall flaws, so surface preparation must be perfect.

Grasscloths are imported wallcoverings that use natural plant fibers. Because they reflect little light, grasscloths soften the appearance of a room. They are a good choice for flawed, irregular walls. Hang them with clear adhesive. Never use water to rinse grasscloths.

Flocked wallcoverings are patterned with raised fibers that suggest the look of velvet. Avoid heavy brushing when hanging flocked wallcoverings, and never use a seam roller.

Fabric wallcoverings are made of woven textiles. Fabrics are easy to hang because there is no pattern to match, but they may be difficult to clean.

Embossed wallcoverings are stamped with a relief pattern for an elegant, formal appearance. Never use a seam roller on embossed wallpapers: they can be easily damaged.

Tips for Choosing Wallcovering

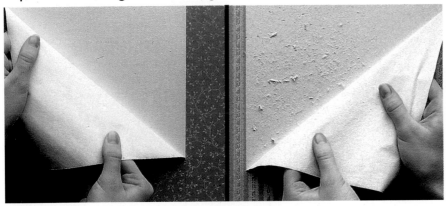

Removability: Strippable wallcoverings (left) can be pulled away from the wall by hand leaving little or no film or residue. Peelable wallcoverings (right) can be removed, but may leave a thin paper layer on the wall, which can usually be removed with soap and water. Check the back of the sample or the wallcovering package for its strippability rating. Choose a strippable product to make future redecorating easier.

Washability: Washable wallcoverings can be cleaned with mild soap and water and a sponge. Scrubbable wallcoverings are durable enough to be scrubbed with a soft brush. Choose scrubbable wallcoverings for any heavy-use areas.

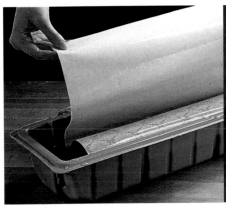

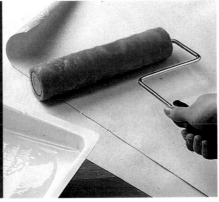

Application: Prepasted wallcoverings (left) are factory-coated with water-base adhesive that is activated when wallcovering is wetted in a water tray. Unpasted wallcoverings (right) must be coated with an adhesive for hanging. As well as being easier to prepare, today's prepasted products are just as durable as those requiring an adhesive coat.

Dye-lot: Jot down dye-lot numbers for reference. If you need additional rolls, order from the same dye-lot to avoid slight color differences.

Packaging: Wallcoverings are sold in continuous triple, double and single-roll bolts.

Patterns: There is always more waste with large patterns. A wallcovering with a large drop pattern can be more expensive to hang than one with a smaller repeat. With large designs, it may also be difficult to avoid obvious pattern interruptions at baseboards or corners.

Measuring & Estimating Wallcovering

With a few room measurements, and the information listed on the wallcovering package, you can estimate the correct amount of wallcovering to buy. The procedure given on these two pages will help you calculate the square footage of your walls and ceilings, and show you how to find the per-roll coverage of wallcovering.

Because of normal trimming waste, the per-roll coverage of wallcovering will be at least 15% less than the coverage listed on the package. The waste percentage can be higher depending on how much space it takes for the wallcovering pattern to repeat itself. This "pattern repeat" measurement is listed on the wallcovering package. You can compensate for this extra waste factor by adding the pattern repeat measurement to the wall height measurement of the room.

Measure the room: Walls: Measure the **length** of the wall, to the nearest ½ foot. (Add length of all walls to find the **perimeter**, if entire room will be wallcovered.) Include window and door openings in wall measurements. Measure the **height** of surfaces to be covered, to nearest ½ foot. Do not include baseboards or crown moldings in height measurement. Ceilings: Measure the **length** and the **width** of the ceiling to the nearest ½ foot.

How to Measure Unusual Surfaces

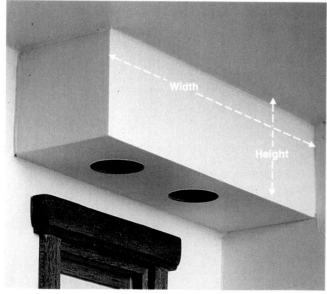

Soffits. If covering all sides of a soffit, add the **width** and **height** into the wall or ceiling measurement.

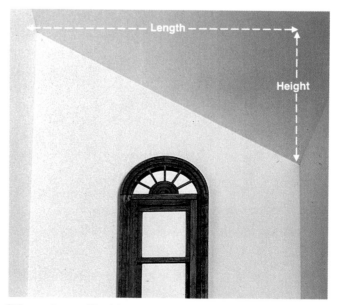

Triangular walls. Measure as though surface is square: length × height.

How to Figure Actual Per-roll Coverage

1) Total per-roll coverage (square feet)	
2) Adjust for waste factor	× .85
3) **Actual Per-roll Coverage** (square feet)	=

How to Calculate Rolls Needed for a Ceiling

1) Room length (feet)	
2) Wallcovering pattern repeat (feet)	+
3) Adjusted length (feet)	=
4) Room width (feet)	×
5) Ceiling area (square feet)	=
6) Actual Per-roll Coverage (figured above; square feet)	÷
7) **Number of Rolls Needed for Ceiling**	=

How to Calculate Rolls Needed for Walls

1) Wall height (feet)	
2) Wallcovering pattern repeat (feet)	+
3) Adjusted height (feet)	=
4) Wall length; or room perimeter (feet)	×
5) Wall area (square feet)	=
6) Actual Per-roll Coverage (figured above; square feet)	÷
7) Number of rolls	=
8) Add 1 roll for each archway or recessed window	+
9) **Number of Rolls Needed for Walls**	=

Wallcovering package or pattern book gives per-roll coverage in square feet, and the drop pattern repeat measurement.

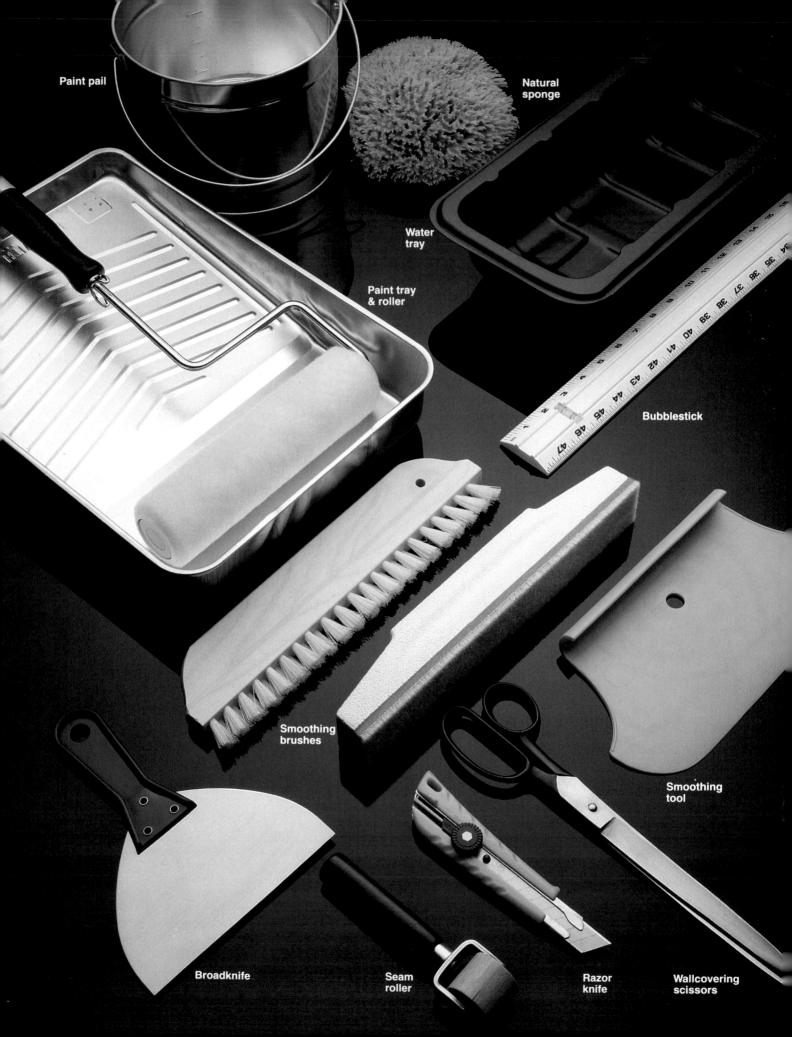

Paint pail

Natural sponge

Water tray

Paint tray & roller

Bubblestick

Smoothing brushes

Smoothing tool

Broadknife

Seam roller

Razor knife

Wallcovering scissors

Tools for Wallcovering

Many of the tools for hanging wallcovering are common items you may already have. Keep a supply of #2 pencils and a pencil sharpener handy for precise marking when laying out and cutting wallcovering. Never use an ink marker or ballpoint pen, because the ink might bleed through the wet wallcovering.

Use a bubblestick or carpenter's level for establishing plumb lines and as a straightedge for cutting. Don't use a chalkline: the chalk can smear the new wallcovering or ooze through the seams. Trim wallcoverings with a razor knife that features breakaway tips. Buy noncorrosive paint pails for holding wash water, and use a natural or high-quality plastic sponge to avoid damaging the wallcovering.

Wallcovering adhesives can be applied with an ordinary paint roller, but you will need a smoothing tool to flatten the wallcovering strips as you hang them, and a seam roller to fix the joints between strips. Ask your dealer about the proper tools for your wallcovering.

Smoothing brushes come in various nap lengths. Use a short nap brush for smoothing out vinyl wallcoverings. A soft, long nap brush is used for fragile wallcoverings, like flocks and grasscloths.

Razor knife with breakaway blade is used for trimming wallcovering at ceiling, baseboard, corners, windows and doors. Renew tips often to avoid snagging and tearing wallcovering.

Wide broadknife holds wallcoverings tightly while trimming overlaps in corners and against window or door casings. A narrower broadknife may work better for intricate corners.

(continued next page)

Wallcovering Tools (continued)

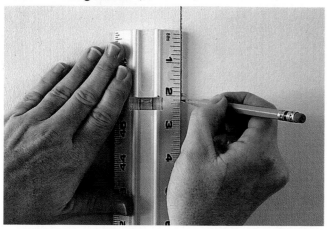

Bubblestick or carpenter's level is used to mark verticals for plumb line, and doubles as a straightedge for marking lines. Use a level instead of a chalk line: chalk can bleed through wallcovering seams.

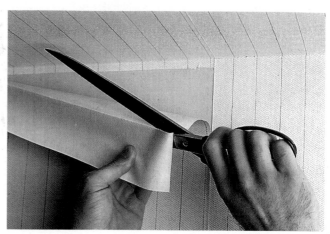

Use wallcovering scissors to trim wallcovering at the seam where wall and ceiling coverings meet. Razor knife may puncture underlying ceiling strip.

Wallcoverer's table provides a flat working surface. Wallcovering stores lend or rent tables, or make your own by placing a sheet of plywood on sawhorses.

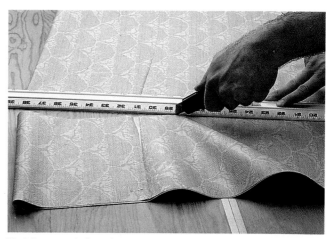

Hold a straightedge tightly against the booked wallcovering strip and cut with a sharp razor knife to form partial strips for corners. Hold knife blade straight while cutting the strip.

Wallcovering tray holds water for wetting prepasted wallcover strips.

Sponge and bucket are used for rinsing down strips. Use a natural or quality synthetic sponge.

Paint roller or paste brush is used to apply adhesive to back of unpasted wallcovering strips.

Materials for Wallcovering

Before hanging wallcovering, the wall surfaces must be both sealed and sized to prevent the adhesives from soaking into the wall surface. Today's premixed primer-sealers do both jobs with a single application.

If your wallcovering is not pre-pasted, you will need one or more types of adhesive. For most vinyl or vinyl-backed wallcoverings, choose a heavy-duty premixed vinyl adhesive that contains a mildew inhibitor. Vinyl wallcoverings also require a special vinyl-on-vinyl adhesive for areas where the wallcovering strips overlap, such as around wall corners and archways.

When hanging specialty wall-coverings, you may need special adhesives. Natural grasscloths, for instance, require a clear-drying adhesive that will not soak through and stain the fibers. Check the wallcovering label or ask your dealer about the correct adhesives for your application.

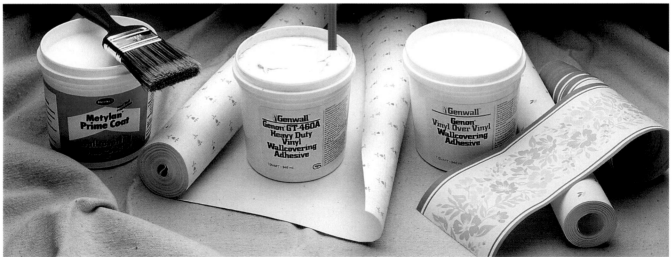

Latex primer-sealer seals and sizes walls in one application. Available as a powder or in pre-mixed form.

Heavy-duty vinyl adhesive is used to hang vinyl or vinyl backed wallcoverings.

Vinyl over vinyl adhesive fastens lap seams on vinyl wallcoverings. Also used to apply vinyl borders over vinyl wallcoverings.

Sketch out seams. Mismatch should be in an inconspicuous area, like behind a door.

The Hanging Plan

Tips for Planning Seams

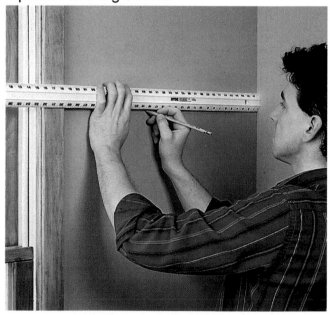

When hanging any patterned wallcovering, there will be one seam where a full strip meets a partial strip. The pattern will usually mismatch at this point. Plan this mismatched seam in an inconspicuous spot, like behind a door or above an entrance.

Sketch out seam lines before you begin. Avoid placing seams that will be difficult to handle. A seam that falls close to the edge of a window or fireplace complicates the job. At corners, wall-covering should always overlap slightly onto the opposite wall. If one or more seams falls in a bad spot, adjust your plumb line a few inches to compensate.

Plan the mismatch. If the room has no obvious focal point, start at the corner farthest from the entry. Measure out a distance equal to wallcovering width and mark a point. Work in both directions, marking out points where the seams will fall.

82

Start at focal point, like a fireplace or large window. Center a plumb line on the focal point, then sketch a wall covering plan in both directions from center line.

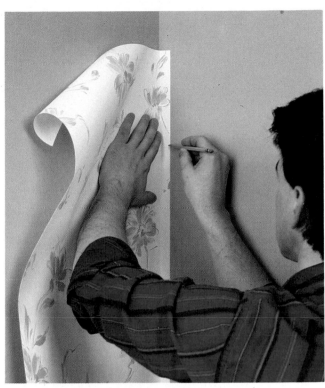

Adjust for corners that fall exactly on seam lines. Make sure you have at least ½" overlap on inside corners, and 1" on outside corners.

Adjust for seams that fall in difficult locations, like near the edge of windows or doors. Shift your starting point so that the seams leave you with workable widths of wallcovering around obstacles.

Plan ceiling so that any pattern interruption will be along the least conspicuous side of the room. Pattern interruptions occur on the last ceiling strip, so begin hanging covering opposite the side where the room is entered.

Reroll each wallcovering roll with pattern side in. Inspect the pattern surface for color and design flaws. Return flawed rolls to your dealer.

Basic Wallcovering Handling Techniques

For durability and easy application, choose a quality prepasted vinyl wallcovering whenever possible. Clear the room of all furniture that can be easily removed, and layer newspapers or drop cloths next to the walls. For easy handling, rent a wallcoverer's table, or use any flat, elevated surface. Shut off electricity, and cover outlet receptacle slots with masking tape to keep out water and adhesive. Work during daylight and make sure each strip is perfectly positioned before going on to the next. Have another person help you, especially when covering ceilings.

Tip: Some premium wallcoverings have unprinted side edges (called "selvages") that protect the roll. The selvages must be cut off the wallcovering strip with a razor knife and straightedge before hanging. The selvages may have printed guide marks for precise cutting.

How to Handle Wallcovering Strips

1 Fill water tray half full of lukewarm water. Roll the cut strip loosely with pattern side in. Wet roll in tray as directed by manufacturer, usually about 1 minute.

How to Measure & Cut Wallcovering Strips

1 Hold wallcovering against wall. Make sure there is a full pattern at the ceiling line, and that wallcovering overlaps ceiling and baseboard by about 2″. Cut strip with scissors.

2 For next strips, find the pattern match with the previously hung strip, then measure and cut new strip with about 2″ excess at each end.

How to Handle Unpasted Wallcovering

2 Holding one edge of the strip with both hands, lift wallcovering from water. Watch pasted side to make sure strip is evenly wetted. Book strip as indicated (page 86).

Lay strip with pattern side down on wallcoverer's table or a flat surface. Apply adhesive evenly to the strip, using a paint roller. Wipe any adhesive from table before preparing next strip.

How to Book Wallcovering Strips

"Book" wallcovering by folding both ends of the strip to center, with pasted side in. Do not crease the folds. Let strip stand (cure) for about 10 minutes. Some wallcoverings should not be booked: follow the manufacturer's directions.

For ceiling strips or wallcovering borders, use an "accordion" book. Fold strip back and forth with pasted side in for easy handling. Let strip stand (cure) for about 10 minutes.

How to Position & Smooth Wallcovering

1 Unfold booked strip and position it lightly with edge butted against plumb line or previous strip. Use flat palms to slide strip precisely into place. Flatten top of strip with a smoothing brush.

2 Beginning at top, smooth wallcovering out from center in both directions. Check for bubbles, and make sure seams are properly butted. Pull strip away and reposition if necessary.

How to Trim Wallcovering

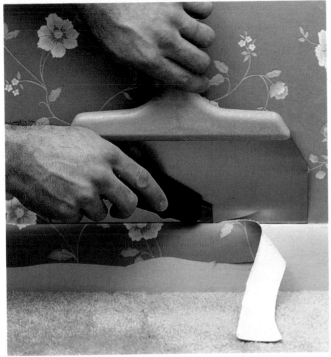

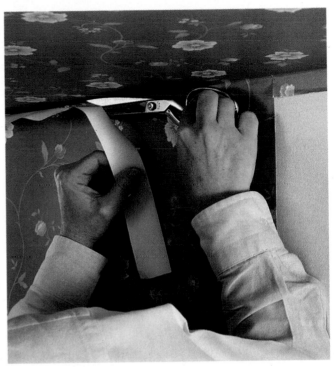

1 Hold wallcovering against molding or ceiling with a wide broadknife. Cut away excess with a sharp razor knife. Keep knife blade in place while changing position of broadknife.

2 With wallcovered ceilings, crease the wall strips with broadknife, then cut along crease with scissors. Cutting with razor knife may puncture ceiling strip.

How to Roll Seams

Let strips stand for about ½ hour. Roll seam gently with seam roller. Do not press out adhesive. Do not roll seams on flocks, foils, fabrics or embossed wall-coverings: tap the seams gently with smoothing brush.

How to Rinse Wallcovering

Use clear water and a sponge to rinse adhesive from surfaces. Change water after every 3 or 4 strips. Do not let water run along seams. Do not use water on grass-cloths, flocks and fabrics.

Hanging Specialty Wallcoverings

Specialty wallcoverings can add new interest to a room, but most require special handling techniques. Reflective wallcoverings, such as foils and mylars, can add light to even the darkest rooms; but the walls must be perfectly smooth before hanging. Fabric or grasscloth wallcoverings can soften and hide flaws in irregular walls, but they are difficult to keep clean.

For very rough walls, consider hanging a liner paper before the wallcovering. Liner paper strips are hung horizontally so that the wallcovering seams cannot overlap the liner seams.

Always follow the manufacturer's directions when hanging specialty wallcoverings, and make your selection carefully: specialty wallcoverings can be expensive.

Special Techniques for Hanging Foils

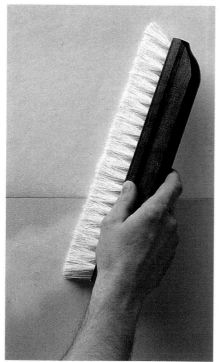

Apply liner paper to create a smooth base for wallcovering over rough or uneven surfaces, such as paneled, textured or masonry walls.

Handle foils carefully. Do not crease or wrinkle the strips, and make sure to flatten out all bubbles immediately when hanging.

Use soft smoothing brush to avoid scratching or burnishing the reflective surface. Do not roll the seams: tap gently with smoothing brush to bond seams.

Special Techniques for Flocks & Fabrics

Use clear adhesive or traditional wheat paste, as directed by manufacturer. Clear adhesive will not bleed through and stain fabric surfaces. Some wallcoverings may direct you to apply adhesive to the walls instead of to the strips.

Use dry paint roller with soft nap, or a soft brush with natural bristles to smooth flocks and fabrics. Stiff smoothing brush bristles might damage the wallcovering surface.

Tap seams with a smoothing brush or your fingers to bond the seams. Do not use a seam roller on flocks, fabrics or other specialty wallcoverings.

Keep adhesive off face of flocks and fabrics, if possible. Remove wet adhesive immediately by blotting with a slightly damp sponge.

Wallcovering Ceilings & Walls

Wallcovering a ceiling is easier if you have another person help you. Let your helper hold one end of the accordion-folded strips.

Dust your hands with talcum powder when handling dry wallcovering, to avoid smudges. When planning a ceiling job, remember that the pattern on the last wallcovering strip may be broken by the ceiling line. Since the least visible ceiling edge is usually on the entry wall, begin hanging ceiling strips at the far end of the room and work back toward the entryway.

If you plan to cover the walls as well as the ceiling, remember that the ceiling pattern can blend perfectly into only one wall. Plan the ceiling job so the strips will blend into your chosen "match" wall.

How to Wallcover a Ceiling

1 Measure width of wallcovering strip and subtract ½". Near corner, measure this distance away from wall at several points, and mark points on ceiling with pencil.

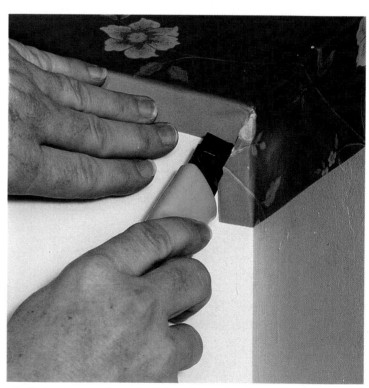

4 Cut out a small wedge of wallcovering in the corner so that strip will lie smooth. Press the wallcovering into the corner with a broadknife.

2 Using marks as guide, draw a guide line along length of ceiling with a pencil and straightedge. Cut and prepare first wallcovering strip (page 84).

3 Working in small sections, position strip against guide line. Overlap side wall by ½", and end wall by 2". Flatten strip with smoothing brush as you work. Trim each strip after it is smoothed.

5 If end walls will also be covered, trim ceiling overlap to ½". Leave ½" overlap on all walls that will be covered with matching wallcovering.

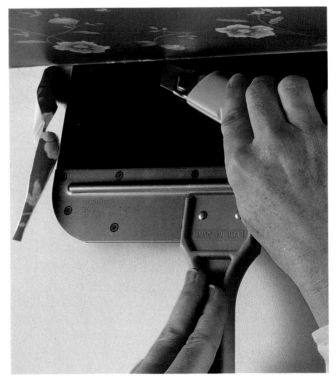

6 On walls that will not be covered, trim excess by holding broadknife against corner and cutting with sharp razor knife. Continue hanging strips, butting edges so that pattern matches.

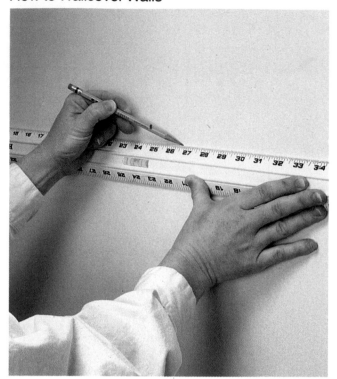

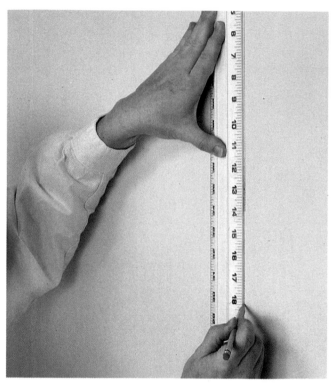

1 Measure from corner a distance equal to the wallcovering width minus ½", and mark a point. Sketch out seam locations, and adjust if necessary (see Hanging Plan, pages 82-83).

2 Draw a plumb line at marked point, using a bubblestick. For wall that must match pattern of wallcovered ceiling, draw the plumb line straight down from first ceiling seam.

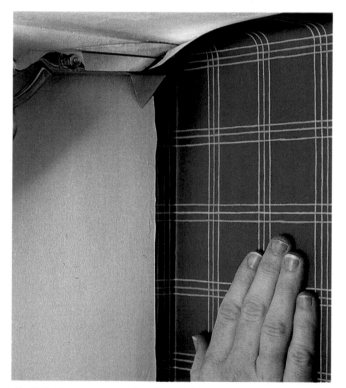

3 Cut and prepare first strip (page 84). First, unfold top portion of booked strip. Position strip against plumb line so that strip overlaps onto ceiling by about 2". Make sure there is a full pattern at ceiling line.

4 Snip top corner of strip so that wallcovering wraps around corner without wrinkles. Use open palms to slide strip into position, with edge butted against plumb line. Press strip flat with smoothing brush.

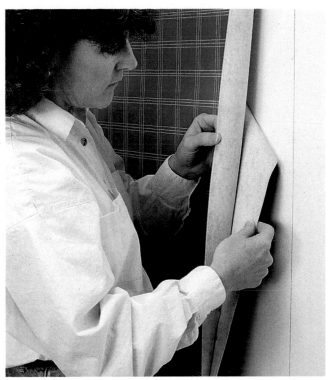

5 Unfold bottom of strip, and use flat palms to position strip against plumb line. Press strip flat with smoothing brush. Check carefully for bubbles.

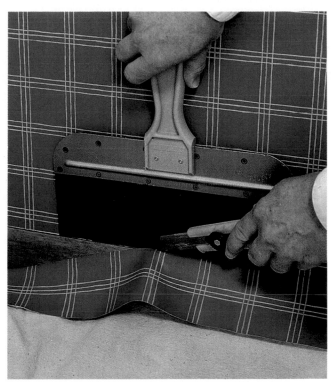

6 Trim excess wallcovering with sharp razor knife. If ceiling is wallcovered, crease edge of wall strip with broadknife, then trim along crease with scissors to avoid punctures. Rinse adhesive off surfaces.

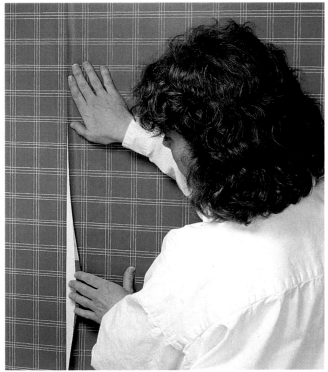

7 Hang additional strips, butting edges so that pattern matches. Let strips stand for about ½ hour, then use a seam roller to lightly roll the seam. On flocks or fabrics, tap the seams gently with smoothing brush.

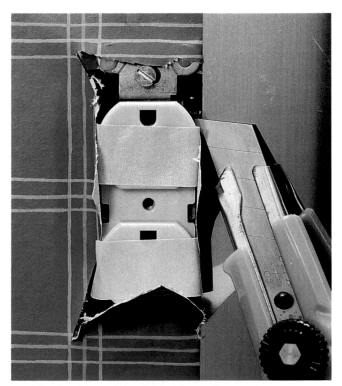

8 With power turned off, hang wallcovering over outlets and switches. Make small diagonal cuts to expose the outlet. Trim wallcovering back to edges of opening with razor knife and broadknife.

How to Wallcover Around an Inside Corner

1 Cut and prepare a full strip (page 84). While strip cures, measure from edge of previous strip to the corner at top, middle, and bottom of wall. Add ½" to longest of these measurements.

2 Align the edges of the booked strip. From the edge, measure at 2 points a distance equal to the measurement found in Step 1. Hold straightedge against the 2 marked points, and cut the wallcovering strip using a sharp razor knife.

3 Position strip on wall with pattern matching the previous strip, overlapping ceiling by about 2". Using open palms, carefully butt edges of strips. Strip will overlap slightly onto uncovered wall.

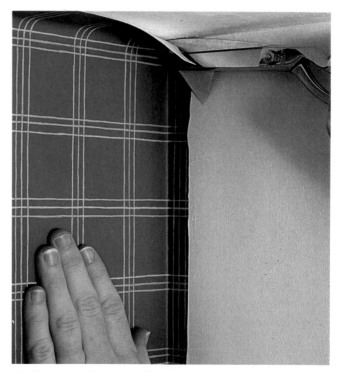

4 Make small corner slits at top and bottom of strip to wrap the overlap around the corner without wrinkles. Flatten strip with smoothing brush, then trim excess at ceiling and baseboard.

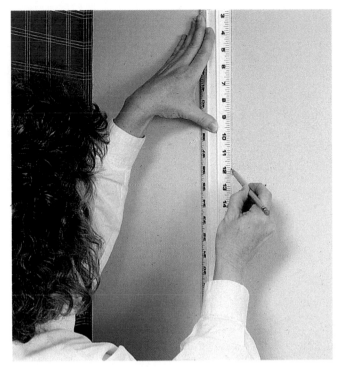

5 Measure width of the remaining strip. Mark this distance from corner onto uncovered wall and mark with pencil. Draw a plumb line from ceiling to floor on new wall, using a bubblestick.

6 Position strip on wall with cut edge toward corner and factory edge against new plumb line. Press the strip flat with a smoothing brush. Trim at ceiling and baseboard.

How to Wallcover Around an Outside Corner

7 If using vinyl wallcovering, peel back edge and apply vinyl-on-vinyl adhesive to lap seam. Press seam area flat. Let strips stand for ½ hour, then roll seams and rinse using a damp sponge.

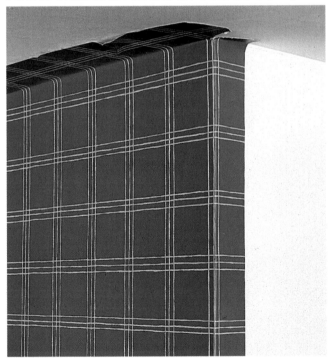

Outside corners can usually be wrapped around without cutting the strip and drawing a new plumb line. If corner is not plumb, follow directions for inside corners, except add 1" to Step 1 measurement to allow for a wider wrap.

Wallcovering Around Windows & Doors

Do not try to precut wallcovering strips to fit the shape of windows or doors. Hang a full strip right over the casing, then smooth the strip before trimming the edges of the door or window. Make diagonal cuts to fit the wallcovering around sharp corners. To avoid damaging the wood on these diagonal cuts, use scissors instead of a razor knife.

If short strips are hung directly above and below opening, make sure these strips are hung exactly vertical to assure a good pattern fit with the next full strip. Do not trim the short strips until the last full strip has been hung. This allows for small adjustments in case of slight mismatches.

How to Wallcover Around Windows & Doors

1 Position strip on wall, directly over window casing. Butt the seam carefully against the edge of the previous strip.

2 Smooth the flat areas of wallcovering with a smoothing brush. Press strip tightly against casing.

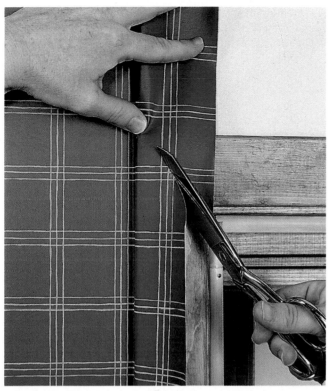

3 Use scissors to cut diagonally from edge of strip to corner of casing. Make similar cut in bottom corner, if hanging around a window.

4 Use scissors to trim away excess wallcovering to about 1" around inside of frame. Smooth wallcovering and press out bubbles as you work.

5 Hold wallcovering against casing with broadknife, and trim excess with sharp razor knife. Trim overlaps at ceiling and baseboard. Rinse wallcovering and casings using a damp sponge.

6 Cut short strips for sections above and below window. You may find scraps that will match the pattern and fit these spaces. Make sure small strips are hung exactly vertical to assure pattern match with the next full strip.

(continued next page)

7 Cut and prepare next full strip. Position it on wall with edge butting previous strip so that the pattern matches.

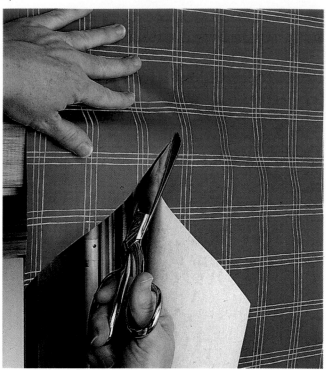

8 Snip top and bottom corners diagonally from edge to corners of casing. Trim away excess wallcovering to about 1" around inside of window or door frame.

9 Match seam on bottom half of strip. Trim excess wallcovering to about 1" with scissors. Flatten strip with smoothing brush.

10 Hold wallcovering against casing with broadknife, and cut excess with sharp razor knife. Trim overlaps at ceiling and baseboard. Rinse wallcovering and casings using a damp sponge.

How to Wallcover a Recessed Window

1 Hang wallcovering strips so they overlap recess. Smooth strips and trim excess at baseboard and ceiling. To wrap top and bottom of recess, make horizontal cut at the halfway point to within ½" of the wall.

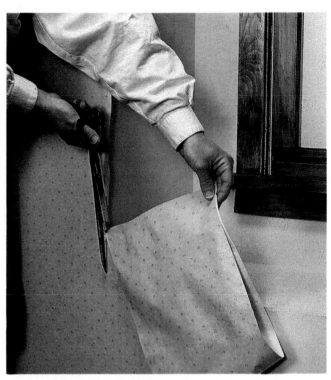

2 From horizontal cut (Step 1), make vertical cuts to top and bottom of recess. Make small diagonal cuts to corners of recess.

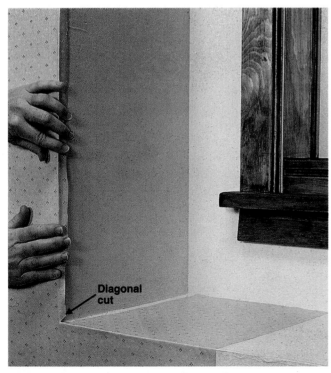

3 Fold the upper and lower flaps of wallcovering onto the recessed surfaces. Smooth the strips and trim at the back edge. Wrap the vertical edge around the corner. Hang wallcovering around window, if needed (pages 96-97).

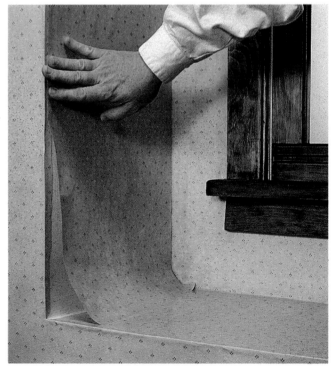

4 Measure, cut and prepare a matching piece of wallcovering to cover side of recess. Side piece should slightly overlap the top and bottom of recess, and the wrapped vertical edge. Use vinyl-on-vinyl adhesive to glue overlapped seams.

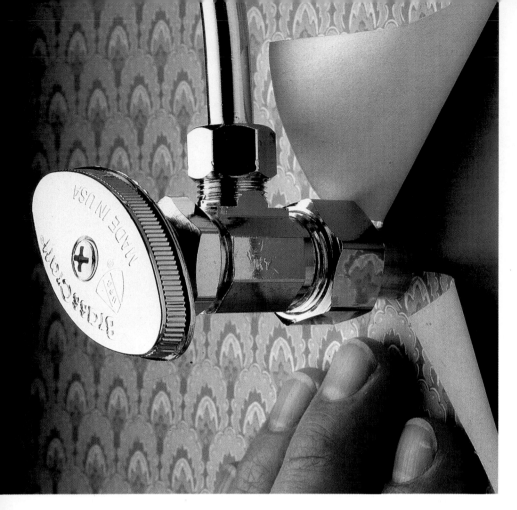

Wallcovering Around Pipes, Radiators & Fixtures

Hanging wallcovering around sinks, pipes and other obstacles requires cutting into wallcovering strips. Hold strip so that patterns match, and cut from the edge closest to the fixture. If possible, cut along a pattern line to hide the slit. At the end of the slit, cut an opening to fit around the fixture. On wall-mounted sinks, tuck small wallcovering overlaps behind the sink.

How to Wallcover Around a Pipe

Escutcheon

1 Pull out escutcheon from wall. Hold wallcovering strip against wall so that pattern matches previous strip. From closest edge of strip, cut slit to reach pipe.

2 Press strip flat up to pipe with a smoothing brush.

3 Cut a hole at the end of the slit to fit around pipe. Butt the edges of slit, and brush smooth.

How to Wallcover Around a Wall-mounted Sink

  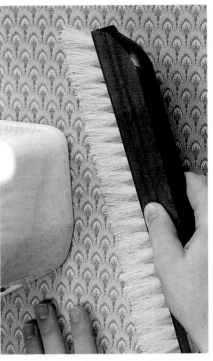

1 Brush wallcovering strip up to edge of sink. Cut horizontal slits in wallcovering, leaving ¼" overlap at top and bottom of sink.

2 Trim wallcovering around side of sink, leaving slight overlap.

3 Smooth wallcovering. Tuck excess wallcovering into crack between sink and wall, if possible, or trim overlap.

How to Wallcover Behind a Radiator

1 Unfold entire strip and position on wall. Smooth strip from ceiling to top of radiator. Use a flat wooden yardstick to lightly smooth the strip down behind the radiator. Crease the wallcovering along baseboard with the yardstick.

2 Pull bottom of strip up from behind radiator. Trim excess wallcovering along crease line. Smooth paper back down behind radiator with yardstick.

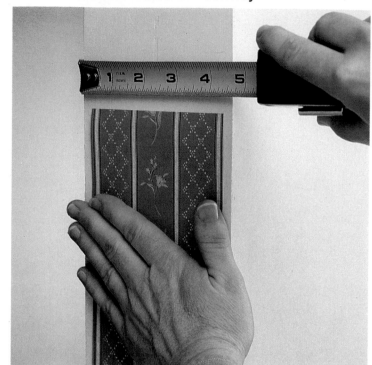

1 Some wallcoverings are available with matching borders that can be used to cover inside of archway. Or, measure inside of archway and cut archway strip from standard wallcovering. Strip should be ¼" narrower than inside surface of archway.

Wallcovering Inside an Archway

Cover the inside surface of an archway with wallcovering after the walls are finished. Wrap the wall strips around the corners of the archway, then hang a matching strip or wallcovering border around the inside surface to cover the wrapped edges. On curved archways, make a series of small slits in the wall strips so that the wallcovering lies smoothly. Use vinyl-on-vinyl adhesive to hang the archway strip.

4 Make small slits in wallcovering along curved portion of archway, cutting as close as possible to wall edge.

102

2 Hang wallcovering on both sides of archway, with strips overlapping archway opening. Smooth the strips and trim excess at ceiling and baseboards.

3 Use scissors to trim overlapping wallcovering, leaving about 1" excess.

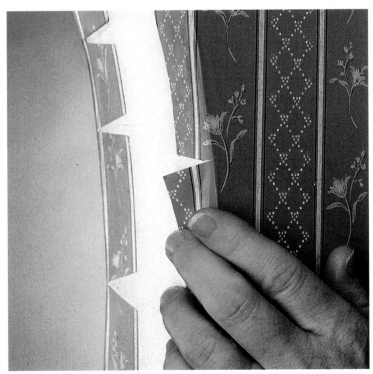

5 Wrap cut edges inside archway and press flat. If adjacent room is to be wallcovered, wrap wallcovering around edge of archway from both sides.

6 Coat back of archway strip with vinyl-on-vinyl adhesive. Position strip along inside of archway with ⅛" space on each edge of strip. Smooth strip with smoothing brush. Rinse strip using damp sponge.

Covering Switch & Outlet Coverplates

As a finishing touch, cover the switch and outlet coverplates with matching wallcovering. For plastic coverplates, use a vinyl-over-vinyl adhesive.

If you wallcover the coverplates in guest bathrooms and bedrooms, you may want to install switches with illuminated levers for the benefit of guests.

Tip: To fully blend switches and outlets with walls, paint receptacle face, switch levers and coverplate screw heads with matching paint.

An easy way to match outlets and switches is to purchase new clear plastic coverplates. Cut wallcovering to fit into the coverplates, and cut openings for switch levers and receptacle faces.

How to Cover Switch or Outlet Coverplates

1 Remove coverplate and reinsert screws. Cut scrap wallcovering that matches area around switch or outlet. Fasten patch over outlet or switch with drafting tape, so that pattern matches wall.

2 Rub surface of patch to emboss outline of outlet or switch screws. Remove patch and mark embossed reference points in pencil on the back side.

3 Lay the coverplate facedown over the wallcovering patch so that outline lines up with holes in coverplate. Mark the corners of the coverplate on the patch.

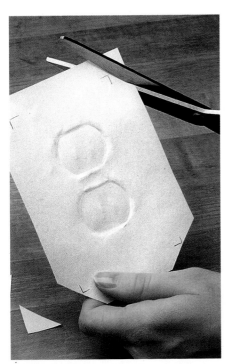

4 Trim scrap ½'' wider than coverplate on all sides. Trim corners of patch, cutting just outside corner marks.

5 Apply vinyl-on-vinyl adhesive to coverplate and patch. Attach coverplate to wallcovering. Smooth out bubbles. Wrap overlap around back and tape edges in place.

6 Use razor knife to cut openings in coverplate. Tape the wallcovering pattern specifications on the back of the coverplate for future reference.

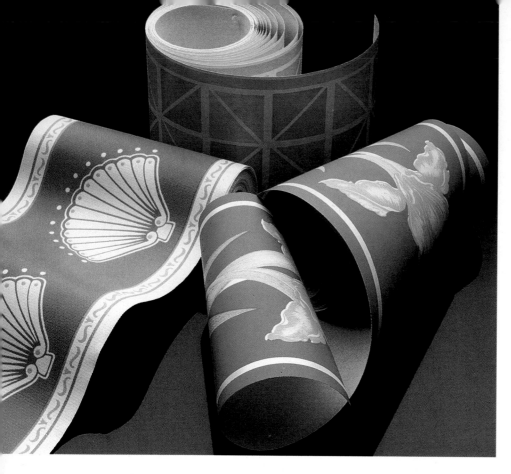

Hanging Wallcovering Borders

Wallcovering borders add an elegant accent to either painted or wallcovered walls. Hang a border as a crown molding around a ceiling, or as a frame around windows, doors or fireplaces.

Use a border along the top of wainscoting, or as an attractive chair rail on painted walls. You can even use a wallcovering border to frame a favorite art piece. Many wallcovering designs have complementary borders which are sold by the linear yard. Or you can create your own border by cutting narrow strips from full-size wallcovering.

How to Hang Borders

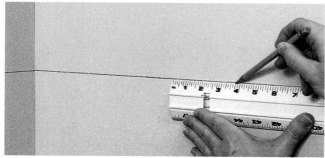

1 Plan starting point so that mismatch seam of border will fall in an inconspicuous area. For chair rail borders, use a level and draw light pencil line around room at desired height.

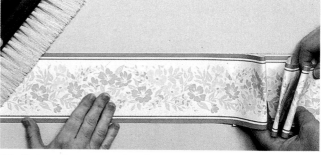

2 Cut and prepare the first strip. Begin at a corner, and overlap border onto adjacent wall by ¼". Have a helper hold the accordion-booked border while you apply and brush it.

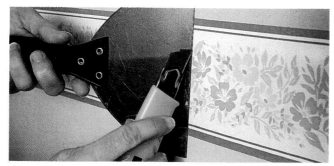

3 For seams that fall in the middle of walls, overlap border strips so that patterns match. Double-cut seam by cutting through both layers with razor knife. Peel back border and remove cut ends. Press border flat.

4 To "cut-in" flush with wallcovering, overlap border onto wallcovering, then use straightedge and razor knife to cut through underlying wallcovering along border edge. Pull up border and remove cut wallcovering. Press border flat.

How to Miter Border Corners

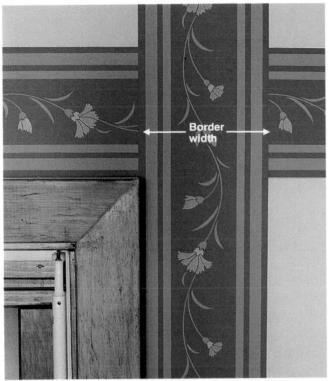

1 Apply horizontal border strips so that they run past the corners with overlap greater than border width. Apply vertical border strips along the side casings, overlapping top and bottom strips.

2 Check position of strip to make sure important pattern designs will remain intact at diagonal cuts. Remove and adjust strips, if necessary.

3 Holding straightedge at 45° angle from casing corner, double-cut both layers with razor knife. Peel back ends of border and remove the cut pieces.

4 Press the border back in place. Let border stand for ½ hour, then lightly roll the seams and rinse the border with damp sponge.

Finishing Touches

After you have finished wallcovering a room, check for final touch-ups while the job is still fresh. Pay special attention to the seams: if you rolled the seams too hard, or rolled them before the adhesive set, you may have squeezed too much adhesive from under the edges of the covering. These edges will look tight while they are wet but will bubble after the covering is dry. Reglue the edges of the seam as shown.

Standing close to the wall, look down its length, against the light. With a strong sidelight you see any bubbles or loose spots in the coverage.

How to Fix a Seam

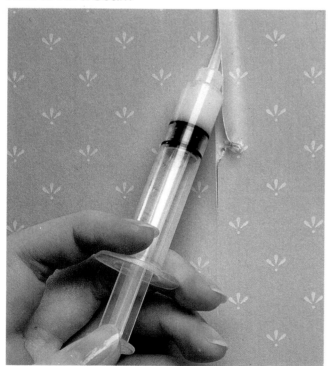

Lift the edge of wallcovering and insert the tip of glue applicator under it. Squirt adhesive onto the wall and gently press the seam flat. Let repair stand for ½ hour, then smooth the seam lightly with a roller. Wipe seam lightly with damp sponge.

How to Fix a Bubble

1 Cut a slit through the bubble using a sharp razor knife. If there is a pattern in the wallcovering, cut along a line to hide the slit.

How to Patch Wallcovering

1 Fasten a scrap of matching wallcovering over the damaged portion with drafting tape, so that the patterns match.

108

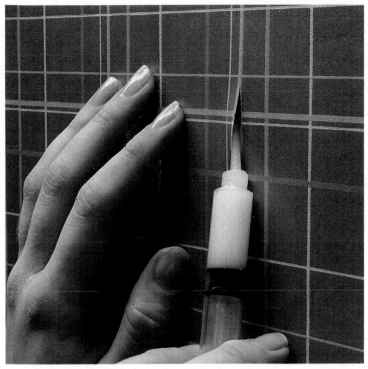

2 Insert the tip of the glue applicator through the slit and apply adhesive sparingly to the wall under the wallcovering.

3 Press wallcovering gently to rebond it. Use a clean damp sponge to press the flap down and wipe away excess glue.

2 Holding razor knife blade at 90° angle to wall, cut through both layers of wallcovering. If wallcovering has strong pattern lines, cut along lines to hide seams. With less definite patterns, cut irregular lines.

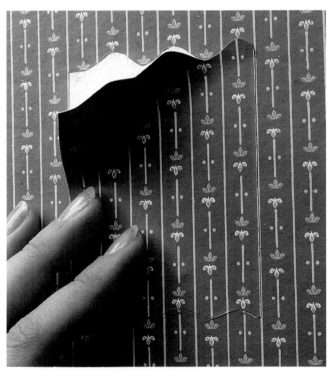

3 Remove the scrap and patch, then peel away the damaged wallcovering. Apply adhesive to the back of the patch and position it in the hole so that pattern matches. Rinse patch area with damp sponge.

DECORATIVE PAINTING TECHNIQUES

Paint finishes add a personal touch to walls and furnishings.

Decorative painting is a creative way to express your individual style and to give walls, furniture, and room accessories a customized finish. Select from a variety of paint finishes that can be used on plaster, wood, metal, ceramic, and fabric.

Select paint finishes that complement your own decorating style. To contrast with sleek contemporary furnishings, apply a faux granite finish to a piece of sculpture. Use faux marble for a lamp that has a Classical influence. Use an alabaster finish for traditional crown moldings or a granite look for plaster statuary and terra-cotta pots.

Try paint glazes to add visual texture. For walls, you may want a mottled finish in tone-on-tone colors. Or make a bolder statement with strié walls in a deep, rich color.

Water-soluble paints of latex and acrylic are used for all the techniques in this book, to make the cleanup easier and to protect the environment. To achieve the different finishes, various paint mediums are often used to either thin or thicken the paints and to extend their drying time.

All information in this book has been tested; however, because skill levels and conditions vary, the publisher disclaims any liability for unsatisfactory results. Follow the manufacturers' instructions for tools and materials used to complete these projects. The publisher is not responsible for any injury or damage caused by the improper use of tools, materials, or information in this publication.

TYPES OF WATER-BASED PAINT

A wide variety of paint is available from paint supply stores and craft stores. Each type has advantages that make it especially suitable for certain kinds of painting. All of the following are water-based, making cleanup easy with soap and water. Water-based paints are also safer for the environment than oil-based paints.

Latex paint is fast drying and durable. In addition to the wide range of premixed colors, latex paint can be custom-mixed by a paint professional. It is available in various finishes, from flat latex for a matte appearance to high-gloss latex with maximum sheen. Low-luster latex enamel paint, sometimes referred to as eggshell enamel, has some sheen and provides good coverage; semigloss has a bit more sheen. The glossier the paint, the more durable it is. Packaged in pints, quarts, and gallons, latex paint is suitable for general use in small and large jobs.

Latex paint contains acrylic or vinyl resins or a combination of both. Latex paints of acrylic resins are the highest quality, with vinyl-acrylic blends next in quality, followed by paints consisting solely of vinyl resins. High-quality paints may cost significantly more, but they provide an even, complete coverage and wear longer.

Aerosol acrylic paints offer excellent coverage and are fast drying. They can be applied quickly and easily without leaving brush marks and are especially convenient for painting textured surfaces that are difficult to paint with a paintbrush. Aerosol acrylic paints are available in a variety of finishes, from matte to high gloss. To protect the environment, select an aerosol paint that does not contain harmful propellants like fluorocarbons or methylene chloride.

Craft acrylic paint contains 100 percent acrylic resins. Generally sold in 2-oz., 4-oz., and 8-oz. bottles or jars, these premixed acrylics have a creamy brushing consistency and give excellent coverage. They should not be confused with the thicker artist's acrylics used for canvas paintings. Craft acrylic paint can be diluted with water, acrylic extender, or latex paint conditioner (page 114) if a thinner consistency is desired. Craft acrylic paints are available in many colors and in metallic, fluorescent, and iridescent formulas.

Ceramic paints provide a scratch-resistant and translucent finish. They can be heat-hardened in a low-temperature oven to improve the paint's durability, adhesion, and water resistance. Latex and acrylic paints may also be used for painting ceramics, provided the surface is properly primed (page 117).

Fabric paints have been formulated specifically for painting on fabric. To prevent excessive stiffness in the painted fabric, avoid a heavy application; the texture of the fabric should show through the paint. Once the paints are heat-set with an iron, the fabric can be machine washed and dry-cleaned. Acrylic paints can also be used for fabric painting; textile medium (page 115) may be added to the acrylics to make them more pliable on fabric.

Paint mediums, such as conditioners, extenders, and thickeners, are often essential for successful results in decorative painting. Available in latex or acrylic, paint mediums are formulated to create certain effects or to change a paint's performance without affecting its color. Some mediums are added directly to the paint, while others are used simultaneously with paint. Mediums are especially useful for latex and acrylic paint glazes (page 129), in that they make an otherwise opaque paint somewhat translucent.

Latex paint conditioner, such as Floetrol®, was developed for use in a paint sprayer with latex paint, but this useful product is also essential in making a paint glaze for faux finishes. When paint conditioner is added to paint, it increases the drying or "open" time and extends the wet-edge time to avoid the look of overlapping. The mixture has a lighter consistency and produces a translucent paint finish. Latex paint conditioner may be added directly to either latex or acrylic paint.

Acrylic paint extender thins the paint, increases the open time, and makes paint more translucent. It is also used for the characteristic veins of marbled faux finishes. When used for veining, acrylic extender is not mixed with the paint, but rather is placed next to it; the paint and the extender are mingled as a feather is passed through them.

Acrylic paint thickener increases the drying time of the paint while it thickens the consistency. Thickener can be mixed directly into either acrylic or latex paint. Small bubbles may appear while mixing, but they will disappear as the paint mixture is applied. Thickener is used for painting techniques that require a paint with more body, such as wood graining, marbling, and combing.

Textile medium is formulated for use with acrylic paint, to make it more suitable for fabric painting. Mixed into the paint, it allows the paint to penetrate the natural fibers of cottons, wools, and blends, creating permanent, washable painted designs. After the fabric is painted, it is heat-set with an iron.

PRIMERS

Some surfaces must be coated with a primer before paint is applied. Primers ensure good adhesion of paint and are used to seal porous surfaces so paint will spread smoothly without soaking in. It is usually not necessary to prime a nonporous surface in good condition, such as smooth, unchipped, previously painted wood or wallboard. Many types of water-based primers are available; select one that is suitable for the type of surface you are painting.

Flat latex primer is used for sealing unfinished wallboard. It makes the surface nonporous so fewer coats of paint are needed. This primer may also be used to seal previously painted wallboard before you apply new paint of a dramatically different color. The primer prevents the original color from showing through.

Latex enamel undercoat is used for priming most raw woods or woods that have been previously painted or stained. A wood primer closes the pores of the wood, for a smooth surface. It is not used for cedar, redwood, and plywoods that contain water-soluble dyes, because the dyes would bleed through the primer.

Rust-inhibiting latex metal primer helps paint adhere to metal. Once a rust-inhibiting primer is applied, water-based paint may be used on metal without causing the surface to rust.

Polyvinyl acrylic primer, or PVA, is used to seal the porous surface of plaster and unglazed pottery, if a smooth paint finish is desired. To preserve the texture of plaster or unglazed pottery, apply the paint directly to the surface without using a primer.

Stain-killing primer seals stains like crayon, ink, and grease so they will not bleed through the top coat of paint. It is used to seal knotholes and is the recommended primer for cedar, redwood, and plywood with water-soluble dyes, because it keeps the bleed from these woods from appearing in the paint finish. This versatile primer is also used as the primer for glossy surfaces like glazed pottery and ceramic, making it unnecessary to sand or degloss the surface.

FINISHES

Finishes are sometimes used over paint as the final coat. They protect the painted surface with a transparent coating. The degree of protection and durability varies, from a light application of matte aerosol sealer to a glossy layer of clear finish.

Clear finish, such as water-based urethanes and acrylics, may be used over paint for a durable finish. As with other products, the glossier the finish, the more washable and scratch-resistant. Clear finish is applied with a brush or sponge applicator. Environmentally safe clear finishes are available in pints, quarts, and gallons at paint supply stores and in 4-oz. and 8-oz. bottles or jars at craft stores.

Aerosol clear acrylic sealer, available in matte or gloss, may be used as the final coat over paint as a protective finish. A gloss sealer also adds sheen and depth to the paint finish for a more polished look. For minimal protection, one light coat is used; several light coats are used for a more durable finish. Avoid applying heavy coats, to avoid dripping or puddling. To protect the environment, select an aerosol sealer that does not contain harmful propellants. Use all aerosol sealers in a well-ventilated area.

TOOLS & SUPPLIES

TAPES

When painting, use tape to mask off any surrounding areas. Several brands are available, varying in the amount of tack, how well they release from the surface without damaging the base coat, and how long they can remain in place before removal. You may want to test the tape before applying it to the entire project. The edge of the tape should be sealed tightly to prevent seepage.

Painter's masking tape **(a)** is one of several products developed especially for use with paint. Painter's tape **(b)** is a wide strip of brown paper with adhesive along one edge. Stencil tape **(c)** is similar to painter's masking tape; it bonds securely to Mylar® stencils, yet does not damage a painted surface.

PAINT ROLLERS

Paint rollers are used to paint an area quickly with an even coat of paint. Roller pads, available in several nap thicknesses, are used in conjunction with roller frames. Use synthetic or lamb's wool roller pads to apply water-based paints.

Short-nap roller pads **(a)** with ¼" to ⅜" nap are used for applying glossy paints to smooth surfaces like wallboard, wood, and smooth plaster.

Medium-nap roller pads **(b)** with ½" to ¾" nap are used as all-purpose pads. They give flat surfaces a slight texture.

Long-nap roller pads **(c)** with 1" to 1¼" nap are used to cover textured areas in fewer passes.

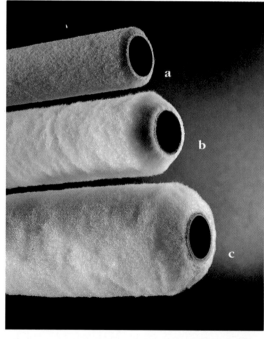

Roller frame is the metal arm and handle that holds the roller pad in place. A wire cage supports the pad in the middle. Select a roller frame with nylon bearings so it will roll smoothly and a threaded end on the handle so you can attach an extension pole.

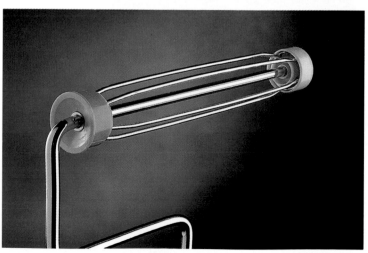

Extension pole has a threaded end that screws into the handle of a roller frame. Use an extension pole when painting ceilings, high wall areas, and floors.

PAINTBRUSHES & APPLICATORS

Several types of paintbrushes and applicators are available, designed for various purposes. Select the correct one to achieve the best quality in the paint finish.

Synthetic-bristle paintbrushes **(a)** are generally used with water-based latex and acrylic paints, while natural-bristle brushes **(b)** are used with alkyd, or oil-based, paints. If natural-bristle paintbrushes are used with water-based paints, the bristles will bunch together. Although this bunching is undesirable for general painting, natural-bristle paintbrushes are intentionally used with water-based paints to create certain decorative effects. For example, natural bristle brushes are used to streak a water-based color-washed finish and for dry brushing water-based paints to soften faux wood and strié finishes.

Brush combs **(c)** remove dried or stubborn paint particles from paintbrushes and align the bristles so they dry properly. To use a brush comb, hold the brush in a stream of water as you pull the comb several times through the bristles from the base to the tips. Use mild soap on the brush, if necessary, and rinse well. The curved side of the tool can be used to remove paint from the roller pad.

Stencil brushes are available in a range of sizes. Use the small brushes for fine detail work in small stencil openings, and the large brushes for larger openings. Either synthetic **(d)** or natural-bristle **(e)** stencil brushes may be used with acrylic paints.

Artist's brushes are available in several types, including fan **(f),** liner **(g),** and flat **(h)** brushes. After cleaning the brushes, always reshape the head of the brush by stroking the bristles with your fingers. Store artist's brushes upright on their handles or lying flat so there is no pressure on the bristles.

Sponge applicators **(i)** are used for a smooth application of paint on flat surfaces.

Paint edgers with guide wheels **(j)** are used to apply paint next to moldings, ceilings, and corners. The guide wheels can be adjusted for proper alignment of the paint pad.

PREPARING THE SURFACE

To achieve a high-quality and long-lasting paint finish that adheres well to the surface, it is important to prepare the surface properly so it is clean and smooth. The preparation steps vary, depending on the type of surface you are painting. Often it is necessary to apply a primer to the surface before painting it. For more information about primers, refer to pages 116 and 117.

PREPARING SURFACES FOR PAINTING

SURFACE TO BE PAINTED	PREPARATION STEPS	PRIMER
UNFINISHED WOOD	1. Sand surface to smooth it. 2. Wipe with tack cloth to remove grit. 3. Apply primer.	Latex enamel undercoat.
PREVIOUSLY PAINTED WOOD	1. Clean surface to remove any grease and dirt. 2. Rinse with clear water; allow to dry. 3. Sand surface lightly to degloss and smooth it and to remove any loose paint chips. 4. Wipe with tack cloth to remove grit. 5. Apply primer to any areas of bare wood.	Not necessary, except to touch up areas of bare wood; then use latex enamel undercoat.
PREVIOUSLY VARNISHED WOOD	1. Clean surface to remove any grease and dirt. 2. Rinse with clear water; allow to dry. 3. Sand surface to degloss it. 4. Wipe with tack cloth to remove grit. 5. Apply primer.	Latex enamel undercoat.
UNFINISHED WALLBOARD	1. Dust with hand broom, or vacuum with soft brush attachment. 2. Apply primer.	Flat latex primer.
PREVIOUSLY PAINTED WALLBOARD	1. Clean surface to remove any grease and dirt. 2. Rinse with clear water; allow to dry. 3. Apply primer, only if making a dramatic color change.	Not necessary, except when painting over dark or strong color; then use flat latex primer.
UNPAINTED PLASTER	1. Sand any flat surfaces as necessary. 2. Dust with hand broom, or vacuum with soft brush attachment.	Polyvinyl acrylic primer.
PREVIOUSLY PAINTED PLASTER	1. Clean surface to remove any grease and dirt. 2. Rinse with clear water; allow to dry thoroughly. 3. Fill any cracks with spackling compound. 4. Sand surface to degloss it.	Not necessary, except when painting over dark or strong color; then use polyvinyl acrylic primer.
UNGLAZED POTTERY	1. Dust with brush, or vacuum with soft brush attachment. 2. Apply primer.	Polyvinyl acrylic primer.
GLAZED POTTERY, CERAMIC & GLASS	1. Clean surface to remove any grease and dirt. 2. Rinse with clear water; allow to dry thoroughly. 3. Apply primer.	Stain-killing primer.
METAL	1. Clean surface with vinegar or lacquer thinner to remove any grease and dirt. 2. Sand surface to degloss it and to remove any rust. 3. Wipe with tack cloth to remove grit. 4. Apply primer.	Rust-inhibiting latex metal primer.
FABRIC	1. Prewash fabric without fabric softener to remove any sizing, if fabric is washable. 2. Press fabric as necessary.	None.

STENCILED DESIGNS

Use stenciled motifs to highlight an area of a room or to simulate architectural details, such as chair rails. A variety of precut stencils is available, with the prices varying widely, usually depending on the intricacy of the design. Or, custom stencils are easily made by tracing designs onto transparent Mylar® sheets. For stencils that coordinate with home furnishings, designs can be adapted from wallpaper, fabric, or artwork. Use a photocopy machine to enlarge or reduce patterns to the desired size.

When stenciling multicolored motifs, it is usually necessary to have a separate stencil for each color. Most precut stencils will have a separate plate for each color and will be numbered according to the sequence for use. A single stencil plate may be used for multiple colors if the spaces between the design areas are large enough to be covered with masking tape. When stenciling multicolored designs, apply the largest part of the design first. When stenciling borders, it is generally best to apply all the repeats of the first color before applying the second color.

Before starting a project, carefully plan the placement of the design. Stencil the design onto paper, and tape it to the surface to check the design placement. Border designs with obvious repeats, such as swags or bows, require careful planning to avoid any partial motifs. If you are stenciling a border, the placement may be influenced by the position of room details, such as windows, doors, and heat vents. It is generally best to start at the most prominent area and work out; the spacing between border repeats may be altered slightly, if necessary.

Use stiff stencil brushes of good quality and sized in proportion to the space being stenciled. Use a separate brush for each color, or clean the brush and allow it to dry before reusing it.

For painting hard surfaces, such as walls and woodwork, use craft acrylic paint mixed with acrylic paint extender, two parts paint to one part extender. This thins the paint and extends the drying time, to allow for more control in shading. You may stencil over a clean, painted surface or over finished wood. If the surface is finished wood, apply a clear finish or sealer to the entire surface after it is stenciled.

For stenciling on fabric, use fabric paints or combine two parts craft acrylic paint to one part textile medium. With either choice of paint, the fabric will not be stiffened. Follow the manufacturer's directions to heat-set the paints. Select fabric that is at least 50 percent cotton, for good penetration of the paint. Avoid fabrics with polished or protective finishes. Prewash fabrics to remove any sizing.

Before beginning the actual project, practice stenciling the designs on paper to become familiar with the way the paint handles and with the shading effects you can achieve.

MATERIALS

GENERAL SUPPLIES

- Precut or custom stencil.
- Craft acrylic paints.
- Acrylic paint extender.
- Stencil brushes.
- Disposable plates.
- Stencil tape.
- Spray adhesive, optional.

FOR CUSTOM STENCILS

- Transparent Mylar sheets.
- Mat knife.
- Cutting surface, such as a self-healing cutting board or cardboard.
- Colored pencils; fine-point permanent-ink marker.

HOW TO MAKE A CUSTOM STENCIL

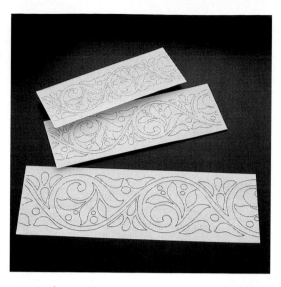

1 Trace design, enlarging or reducing it, if desired. Repeat the design for 13" to 18" length, making sure the spacing between repeats is consistent.

2 Color the traced design as desired, using colored pencils. Mark placement lines so stencil will be correctly positioned on wall.

3 Position Mylar® sheet over traced design, allowing at least 1" border at top and bottom; secure with stencil tape. Trace areas that will be stenciled in first color, using marking pen; transfer placement lines.

4 Trace design areas for each additional color on a separate Mylar sheet. To help align the design, outline areas for previous colors, using dotted lines.

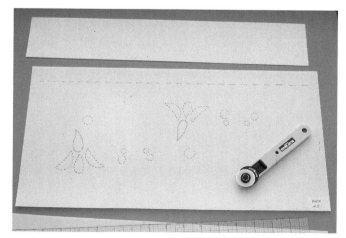

5 Layer the Mylar sheets, and check for accuracy. Using mat knife and straightedge, cut outer edges of the stencil plates, leaving 1" to 3" border around the design.

6 Cut out marked areas on each sheet, using a mat knife; cut the smallest shapes first, then larger ones. Pull knife toward you as you cut, turning the Mylar sheet, rather than the knife, to change the direction.

HOW TO STENCIL ON WALLS, WOOD & OTHER HARD SURFACES

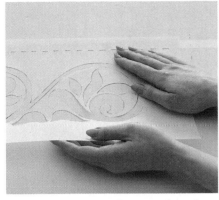  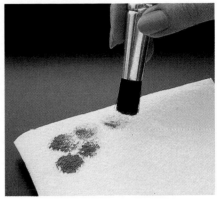

1 Mark placement for stencil on the surface with stencil tape. Position first stencil plate, aligning placement tape with dotted line. Secure the stencil, using stencil tape or spray adhesive.

2 Mix together two parts craft acrylic paint and one part acrylic paint extender on disposable plate.

3 Dip tip of stencil brush into paint mixture. Using a circular motion, blot brush onto folded paper towel until bristles are almost dry.

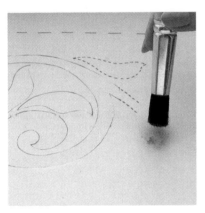  

4 Hold brush perpendicular to surface. Blot brush on blank area of stencil plate, using a light circular stroke; if brush strokes are noticeable, blot the brush on a paper towel again, to remove more of the paint.

5 **Circular method**. Hold the brush perpendicular to the surface, and apply paint, using circular motion, within cut areas of stencil. This gives a blended coverage of paint on hard surfaces, such as walls and wood.

5 Stippling method. Apply masking tape around bristles, ¼" from the end. Hold the brush perpendicular to surface, and apply paint using up-and-down motion. This gives a textured appearance on hard surfaces; it is also the technique to use for fabrics.

6 Stencil all cut areas of first stencil plate; allow to dry. Remove plate. Secure second plate to surface, matching the design. Apply second color in all cut areas. Repeat for any remaining stencil plates until design is completed.

 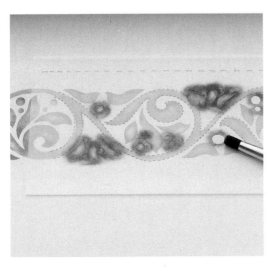 

7 Touch up any glitches or smudges on surface, using background paint and an artist's brush.

MORE IDEAS FOR STENCILED DESIGNS

Tray *is stenciled with a Southwestern motif of red peppers.*

Column and baseboards *are stenciled with coordinating designs for a unified effect.*

Architectural details *are enhanced with the use of stenciled borders.*

Country chair *features coordinating stencil designs on the wooden chair back and fabric seat cushion.*

Fireplace screen *features an elaborate stencil of chestnut leaves.*

PAINTING WITH GLAZES

Many types of decorative painting require the use of a paint glaze, made by adding paint conditioner (page 114) or paint thickener (page 115) to the paint. With these paint mediums, the drying time of the paint is extended, allowing the additional time needed to manipulate the paint before it sets. The glaze has a creamy texture when wet and forms a translucent top coat once it dries.

Paint glazes were formerly made from oil-based paints mixed with oil glaze. These oil glazes were messy to use, difficult to clean up, and noxious. Water-based latex and acrylic glazes, on the other hand, are easier to use, safer for the user and the environment, and lower in cost.

In this section, the basic glaze (below, right) is used for several types of decorative painting, including strié, combing, rag rolling, texturizing, and sometimes, sponging. The glaze is varied slightly for color washing (page 144), antiquing, faux wood grain, and faux moiré. Without the use of paint glazes, all of these finishes would be nearly impossible to achieve.

TECHNIQUES FOR PAINTING WITH GLAZE

Strié (page 130) is the striped effect achieved when a natural-bristle paintbrush is dragged through a wet coat of paint glaze.

Combing also produces a striped effect when a comb is run through wet glaze. For this technique, you may use one of the combing tools available from craft and art stores, or make a comb by cutting V grooves into a rubber squeegee or a piece of mat board. Use the basic glaze for combing, or, for more distinct lines and a more opaque effect, use a thickened glaze.

Rag rolling (page 133) creates an allover mottled look. Different effects can be achieved, depending on which method is used. In the "ragging-on" method, a rag is dipped into the paint glaze, wrung out, and rolled in a random pattern across a surface that has a base coat of paint. In the "ragging-off" method, a coat of paint glaze is applied over a base coat; then a rag is rolled through the wet glaze to form patterns.

Texturizing (page 136) uses a number of household items that can be dragged, blotted, stippled, or rolled to create a pattern with glaze. Some possible items include corrugated cardboard, cheesecloth, plastic wrap, and crumpled paper. As with ragging-on and ragging-off, you can either apply the glaze directly to the item and then onto the base-coated surface, or you can move the item through a coat of wet glaze applied over a base coat of paint.

Paint finishes using glaze include combing (orange), rag rolling (green), texturizing (purple), and strié (gold).

TIPS FOR USING PAINT GLAZE

Use a paint roller to apply the glaze when even coverage is desired or when painting a large surface, such as a wall.

Use a paintbrush to apply the glaze when a paint finish with more variation and pattern in the surface is desired or when painting a small item.

Use a sponge applicator to apply the glaze when smooth coverage is desired or when painting a small item.

Manipulate the glaze while it is still wet. Although humidity affects the setting time, the glaze can usually be manipulated for a few minutes.

Work with an assistant when using glaze on a large surface. While one person applies the glaze, the other can manipulate it.

Protect the surrounding area with a drop cloth or plastic sheet and wear old clothing, because working with glaze can be messy.

Use wide painter's tape (page 118) to mask off the surrounding surfaces. Firmly rub the edges of the tape, to ensure that the glaze will not seep under it.

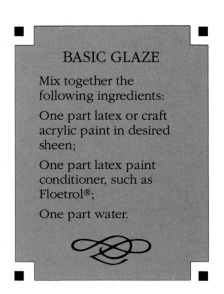

BASIC GLAZE

Mix together the following ingredients:

One part latex or craft acrylic paint in desired sheen;

One part latex paint conditioner, such as Floetrol®;

One part water.

STRIÉ

Strié is a series of irregular streaks in a linear pattern, created by using a paint glaze. Especially suitable for walls, this painting technique can also be used for furniture pieces with flat surfaces.

For this technique, use the basic glaze and instructions on page 129. To achieve the strié effect, pull a dry, wide natural-bristle paintbrush through the glaze while it is wet. Before the glaze completely sets, the lines can be softened by lightly dry-brushing the surface with a soft natural-bristle paintbrush.

For large surfaces, it is helpful to work with an assistant. After one person has applied the glaze, the other person brushes through the glaze before it dries, to achieve the strié effect. If you are working alone, limit yourself to smaller sections, if possible, since the glaze must be wet to create this look. If it is necessary to interrupt the process, stop only when a section is completed.

Because it can be messy to apply a strié finish, wear old clothing and protect the surrounding area with drop cloths and wide painter's tape. Firmly rub the edges of the tape, to ensure that the glaze will not seep under it.

Strié lends itself well to tone-on-tone colorations, such as ivory over white or tones of blue, although the color selection is not limited to this look. To become familiar with the technique and test the colors, first apply the finish to a sheet of cardboard, such as mat board.

HOW TO APPLY A STRIÉ PAINT FINISH

MATERIALS

- Low-luster latex enamel in desired color, for the base coat.
- Latex paint in desired sheen and color, for the glaze.
- Latex paint conditioner, such as Floetrol®.
- Wide natural-bristle brush.
- Soft natural-bristle paintbrush.

1 Prepare surface (page 120). Apply base coat of low-luster latex enamel; allow to dry. Mix glaze (page 129); apply over base coat in a vertical section about 18" wide, using paint roller or natural-bristle paintbrush.

2 Drag a dry, wide natural-bristle paintbrush through wet glaze, immediately after glaze is applied; work from top to bottom in full, continuous brush strokes. To keep brush rigid, hold bristles of brush against surface with handle tilted slightly toward you. Repeat until desired effect is achieved.

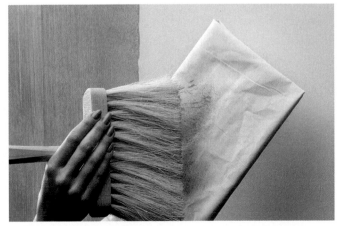

3 Wipe the paintbrush occasionally on clean, dry rag to remove excess glaze, for a uniform strié look. Or rinse brush in clear water, and wipe dry.

4 Brush surface lightly after glaze has dried for about 5 minutes, if softer lines are desired; use soft natural-bristle brush, and keep brush strokes in same direction as streaks.

RAG ROLLING

Rag rolling is a painting technique that gives a rich, textural look with an allover mottled effect. It works well for walls and other flat surfaces, such as dresser tops and drawers, shelves, bookends, and doors. The basic paint glaze on page 129 can be used in either of the two techniques for rag rolling, *ragging-on* and *ragging-off.*

In ragging-on, a rag is saturated in the prepared paint glaze, wrung out, rolled up, and then rolled across a surface that has been base-coated with low-luster latex enamel paint. Rag-on a single application of glaze over the base coat, for a bold pattern. Or, for a more subtle, blended look, rag-on two or more applications of glaze.

In ragging-off, apply a coat of paint glaze over the base coat, using a paintbrush or paint roller; then roll up a rag and roll it over the wet glaze to remove some of the glaze. This process may be repeated for more blending, but you must work fast, because the glaze dries quickly.

If you are using the ragging-off method on large surfaces, such as walls, it is helpful to have an assistant. After one person applies the glaze, the second person can rag-off the area before the glaze dries. While it is not necessary to complete the entire room in one session, it is important that you complete an entire wall.

With either method, test the technique and the colors that you intend to use on a large piece of cardboard, such as mat board, before you start the project. Generally, a lighter color is used for the base coat, with a darker color for the glaze.

Feel free to experiment with the technique as you test it, perhaps rag rolling two different glaze colors over the base coat. Or try taping off an area, such as a border strip, and rag rolling a second or third color within the taped area.

Because the glaze can be messy to work with, apply a wide painter's tape around the area to be painted and use drop cloths to protect the surrounding surfaces. Wear old clothes and rubber gloves, and keep an old towel nearby to wipe your hands after you wring out the rags.

MATERIALS

- Low-luster latex enamel paint, for base coat.
- Latex or craft acrylic paint and latex paint conditioner, for glaze; 1 qt. of each is sufficient for the walls of 12 ft. × 14 ft. room.
- Paint pail; rubber gloves; old towel; lint-free rags, about 24" square.

Rag rolling *adds textural interest to walls, furniture, and accessories. Opposite, ragging-on was used for the walls, while ragging-off was used for the vase. The tabletop above was painted by ragging-off.*

HOW TO APPLY A RAG-ROLLED PAINT FINISH USING THE RAGGING-ON METHOD

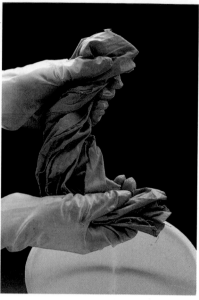

1 Prepare surface (page 120). Apply a base coat of low-luster latex enamel, using paintbrush or paint roller. Allow to dry.

2 Mix basic glaze (page 129) in pail. Dip lint-free rag into glaze, saturating entire rag; wring out well. Wipe excess glaze from hands with old towel.

3 Roll up the rag irregularly; then fold in half to a width equal to both hands.

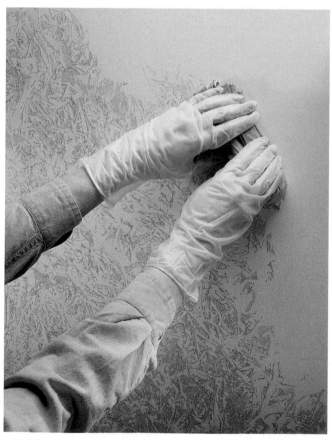

4 Roll the rag over surface, working upward at varying angles. Rewet rag whenever necessary, and wring out.

5 Repeat the application, if more coverage is desired.

HOW TO APPLY A RAG-ROLLED PAINT FINISH
USING THE RAGGING-OFF METHOD

1 Apply base coat of low-luster latex enamel, using paintbrush or paint roller. Allow to dry.

2 Mix basic glaze (page 129); pour into a paint tray. Apply the glaze over the base coat, using paint roller or paint pad.

3 Roll up lint-free rag irregularly; fold in half to width of both hands. Roll the rag through the wet glaze, working upward at varying angles.

COLOR EFFECTS

As shown in the examples below, the color of the base coat is not affected when the ragging-on method is used. With the ragging-off method, the color of the base coat is changed, because the glaze is applied over the entire surface, and then some glaze is removed with a rag to soften the background.

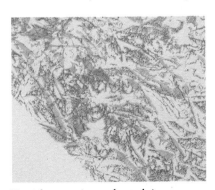

Ragging-on is used, applying aqua glaze over a white base coat. The white base coat remains unchanged.

Ragging-off is used, applying aqua glaze over a white base coat. The white base coat is covered with the glaze, then appears as a lighter aqua background when some of the glaze is removed.

Ragging-on and ragging-off are both used. First a taupe glaze is ragged-on over a white base coat. Then a rust glaze is ragged-off, changing the white base coat to a lighter shade of rust.

TEXTURIZING

There are several ways to achieve a finish that has visual texture with paint glaze in addition to the methods for strié, combing, and rag rolling, using any number of household items and painting supplies. Rolled or bent pieces of corrugated cardboard, cheesecloth, crumpled paper, raffia, plastic wrap, carved potatoes, and scrub brushes create interesting textured effects. The list of items is as endless as your imagination.

For these finishes, use the basic glaze and instructions on page 129. You may apply a coat of glaze directly to the surface, then manipulate it or partially remove it by dabbing the glaze with the item or items you have selected. Or using the alternate method, the glaze may be applied to the selected items, then printed onto the surface. To become familiar with the methods and determine which effects you prefer, experiment with both methods, using a variety of items.

Apply a base coat of paint, using a good-quality low-luster latex enamel, before you apply the glaze. The base coat and the glaze may be in contrasting colors, such as emerald green over white. For a more subtle look, try a tone-on-tone effect, such as two shades of blue, or choose colors that are similar in intensity, such as deep red over deep purple. For even more possibilities, the process can be repeated, using one or more additional colors of glaze. This adds even more visual interest and is especially suitable for small accessories.

MATERIALS

- Low-luster latex enamel paint in desired color, for base coat.
- Latex paint in desired sheen and color, for glaze.
- Latex paint conditioner, such as Floetrol®.
- Items selected for creating the textural effect.

Accessories (above) have a variety of textural effects, created using folded cheesecloth for the vase, rolled corrugated cardboard for the bowl, and single-face corrugated cardboard for the tray.

Folding screen (opposite) features three texturizing methods. For the background, plastic wrap was used to remove some of the glaze. For the border insert at the top, a fan brush was used to apply glaze. For the center inserts, crumpled paper was used to apply glaze.

1 Prepare surface (page 120). Apply a base coat of low-luster latex enamel, using sponge applicator, paintbrush, or paint roller. Allow to dry.

2 Mix glaze (page 129). Apply glaze to a small area at a time, using sponge applicator, paintbrush, or paint roller. A heavier coat of glaze gives a more opaque finish, and a light coat, a more translucent finish.

3 Texturize glaze by dabbing, rolling, or dragging items in the glaze to create patterns; rotate item, if desired, to vary the look. Replace the item as necessary, or wipe the excess glaze from item occasionally.

Alternate method. Follow step 1, above. Then apply glaze to selected item, using a sponge applicator, paintbrush, or paint roller; blot on paper towel or cardboard. Dab, roll, or drag glaze-covered item over base coat, to apply glaze to surface randomly or in desired pattern.

SUGGESTED TECHNIQUES FOR TEXTURIZING

Rolled corrugated cardboard is secured by taping it together. Use corrugated end to make designs in coat of wet glaze (left). Or apply glaze directly to cardboard; blot, and print designs on surface (right).

Single-face corrugated cardboard is cut to the desired shape. To make designs, press corrugated side in coat of wet glaze (left). Or apply glaze directly to corrugated side; blot, and print designs on surface (right).

Cheesecloth is folded into a flat pad and pressed into coat of wet glaze (left). Or apply glaze directly to a folded flat pad of cheesecloth, then imprint the cheesecloth onto the surface (right).

Plastic wrap is wrinkled slightly and placed over coat of wet glaze; press lightly, and peel off (left). Or apply glaze directly to plastic wrap. Then place plastic wrap on the surface, folding and crinkling it; peel off (right).

Crumpled paper is pressed into coat of wet glaze (left). Or apply glaze directly to paper; press onto the surface, crumpling the paper (right).

Fan brush is pressed into wet glaze, making uniform rows of fan-shaped impressions (left). Or apply glaze directly to fan brush, and print fan-shaped designs on surface (right).

SPONGE PAINTING

Sponge painting produces a soft, mottled effect and is one of the easiest techniques to use. To achieve this paint finish, use a natural sea sponge to dab paint onto a surface. Cellulose or synthetic sponges should not be used, because they tend to leave identical impressions with hard, defined edges.

The sponged look can be varied, depending on the number of paint colors applied, the sequence in which you apply the colors, and the distance between the sponge impressions. You can use semigloss, low-luster, or flat latex paint for the base coat and the sponging. Or for a translucent finish, use a paint glaze that consists of paint, paint conditioner, and water; make the glaze as on page 129.

To create stripes, borders, or panels, use painter's masking tape to mask off the desired areas of the surface after the first color of sponged paint is applied. Then apply another color to the unmasked areas.

MATERIALS

- Craft acrylic or latex paints in desired sheens and colors, for base coat and for sponging.
- Natural sea sponge.
- Painter's masking tape.
- Carpenter's level, for painting stripes, borders, or panels.

Napkin *has been sponge painted, using fabric paints instead of latex or craft acrylic paints. For sponge painting on fabrics, do not blend the colors with a wet sponge.*

Urn and wall *(opposite) show two different applications for sponge painting. The urn is sponged following its swirled design lines; for sheen, gold metallic paint was applied last. The wall is sponge painted in stripes as on page 143.*

1 Prepare surface (page 120). Apply base coat of desired color. Allow to dry. Rinse sea sponge in water to soften it; squeeze out most of the water. Saturate sponge with paint or with paint glaze (page 129). Blot the sponge lightly on paper towel.

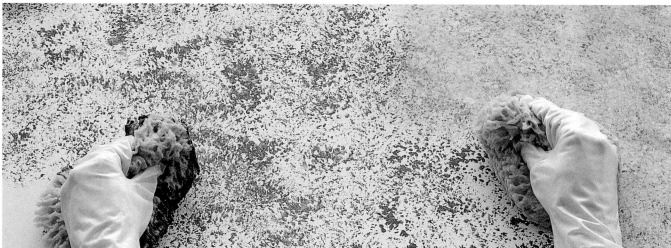

2 Press sponge repeatedly onto surface, as shown at left; work quickly in small areas, and change position of sponge often. Blot paint on surface immediately, using wet sea sponge in other hand, as shown at right; this causes the paint to bleed, for a softened, blended look. Some of the paint is removed with the wet sponge.

3 Continue to apply the first paint color to entire project, blotting with moist sponge. Repeat steps with one or more additional colors of paint, if desired. Allow paint to dry between colors.

4 **Optional feathering.** Apply final color of paint, using a light, sweeping motion instead of dabbing.

HOW TO SPONGE PAINT STRIPES, BORDERS, OR PANELS

1 Follow steps 1 to 3, opposite. Allow paint to dry thoroughly. Mark light plumb line, using a pencil and carpenter's level. Position first row of painter's masking tape along this line.

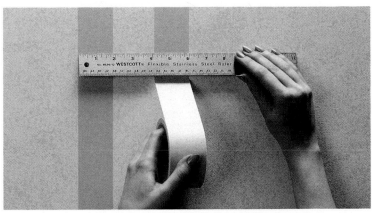

2 Measure and position remaining rows of painter's masking tape to mark stripes, borders, or panel areas.

3 Apply second paint color to the unmasked areas of the surface. Allow paint to dry.

4 Remove the painter's masking tape, revealing two variations of sponge painting.

COLOR EFFECTS

When related colors are used for sponge painting, such as two warm colors or two cool colors, a harmonious look is achieved. For a bolder and more unexpected look, sponge paint in a combination of warm and cool colors.

Warm colors like yellow and orange blend together for an exciting effect.

Cool colors like green and blue blend together for a tranquil effect.

Warm and cool colors like yellow and blue combine boldly, but sponge painting softens the effect.

COLOR WASHING

Color washing is an easy paint finish that gives walls a translucent, watercolored look. It adds visual texture to flat drywall surfaces, and it further emphasizes the already textured surface of a plaster or stucco wall.

In this technique, a color-washing glaze is applied in a cross-hatching fashion over a base coat of low-luster latex enamel, using a natural-bristle paintbrush. As the glaze begins to dry, it can be softened further by brushing the surface with a dry natural-bristle paintbrush. Complete one wall before moving on to the next or before stopping. Store any remaining glaze in a reclosable container between painting sessions.

The color-washing glaze can be either lighter or darker than the base coat. For best results, use two colors that are closely related or consider using a neutral color like beige or white for either the base coat or the glaze. Because the glaze is messy to work with, cover the floor and furniture with drop cloths and apply painter's tape along the ceiling and moldings.

COLOR-WASHING GLAZE

Mix together the following ingredients:

One part flat latex paint;

One part latex paint conditioner;

Two parts water.

HOW TO COLOR WASH WALLS

MATERIALS

- Low-luster latex enamel paint, for base coat.
- Flat latex paint, for color-washing glaze.
- Latex paint conditioner, for color-washing glaze.
- Paint roller.
- Two 3" to 4" natural-bristle paintbrushes for each person.
- Drop cloths; painter's tape.

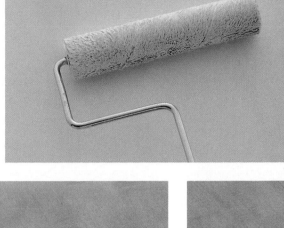

1 Prepare surface (page 120). Apply a base coat of low-luster latex enamel paint in the desired color, using paint roller. Allow to dry.

2 Mix the color-washing glaze, opposite. Dip paintbrush into the glaze; remove excess glaze against rim of the container. Apply the glaze to wall in cross-hatching manner, beginning in one corner. The more you brush over the surface, the softer the appearance.

3 Brush over the surface, if desired, using a dry natural-bristle paintbrush, to soften the look. Wipe excess glaze from the brush as necessary.

COLOR EFFECTS

Select colors for the base coat and the glaze that are closely related, or use at least one neutral color. A darker glaze over a lighter base coat gives a mottled effect. A lighter glaze over a darker base coat gives a chalky or watercolored effect.

Apply darker top coat, such as a medium turquoise, over lighter base coat, such as white.

Apply a lighter top coat, such as white, over a darker base coat, such as coral.

Apply two shades of a color, such as a medium blue top coat over a light blue base coat.

FAUX GRANITE

To duplicate the look of natural granite is very easy. By combining the techniques of sponge painting and specking, you can create a simulated granite that is so realistic that people may actually have to touch it before they realize it is a faux finish.

Natural granite is formed from molten stone and has a crystalline appearance. Granite colors from different regions of the world vary greatly, depending on how fast the molten lava cooled. The most common types of granite in America are composed of earth tones in burnt umber, raw umber, warm gray, black, and white. Some exotic granites consist of a rich combination of burgundy, purple, black, and gray; a fiery mix of copper, umber, black, and gray; the cool opalescence of metallic blue, black, pearl, and gray; and a warm combination of orange, red, and salmon. The color combinations for the granites shown here are given on page 149.

Since this is painted granite, the color combinations need not be realistic. You can use this technique in any color combination, to suit a particular decorating scheme.

Metal lamp and wooden frame *are finished in two coordinating colors of granite.*

Molded plastic boxes, *inexpensive to purchase, are transformed into rich-looking accesssories.*

Plaster pedestal, *finished in faux granite, becomes the base for a glass-top table.*

HOW TO APPLY A FAUX GRANITE PAINT FINISH

MATERIALS

- Flat latex or craft acrylic paint, for base coat.
- Flat latex or craft acrylic paint in desired colors, for sponging and specking; metallic paint may be used for one of the colors.
- Natural sea sponge.
- Fine-bristle scrub brush or toothbrush.
- Low-luster aerosol clear acrylic sealer or clear finish.

1 Prepare surface (page 120). Apply a base coat of flat latex or craft acrylic paint in white, gray, or black.

2 Dilute one paint color for sponging, one part paint to one part water, or to the consistency of ink; it may not be necessary to dilute metallic paint. Apply paint to surface in an up-and-down motion, using sea sponge.

3 Blot paint evenly with a clean, dampened sea sponge, immediately after applying it. This mottles the paint, blends it slightly with background color, and increases transparency. If the effect is not pleasing, wipe it off with a damp cloth before it dries.

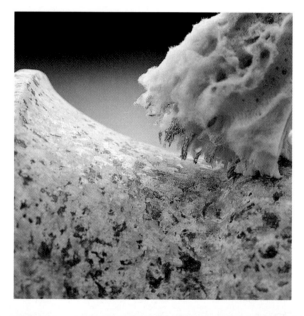

4 Repeat steps 2 and 3 for remaining colors of paint for sponging, allowing each color to dry before the next color is applied. Allow some of the base coat to show through the other layers, to create depth.

5 Apply diluted white, gray, or black paint to surface, using the specking technique, opposite. Speck the surface evenly in a light or moderate application.

6 Apply a low-luster aerosol clear acrylic sealer or clear finish to add sheen and depth and increase durability.

HOW TO ADD SPECKING

1 Dilute the paint for specking with water as in step 2, opposite. Test the paint consistency and technique by specking on cardboard before specking the actual project. Dip the bristles of a fine-bristle scrub brush or a toothbrush into the paint mixture. Dab once on a dry paper towel, to remove excess moisture and prevent drips.

2 Hold the brush next to surface; run craft stick or finger along bristles, causing specks of paint to spatter onto surface. Experiment with how fast you move the craft stick and how far away you hold the brush. Too much paint on the brush may cause paint to drip or run.

COLOR EFFECTS

Granite colors vary from one part of the world to another. Use the color combinations below to simulate some of the natural granites that exist.

Apply a black base coat. Use sea sponge to apply paints in medium gray, light gray, and metallic silver. Speck with more light gray paint.

Apply a dark ivory base coat. Use a sea sponge to apply paints in brown, medium gray, dark gray, and black. Speck with more black paint.

Apply a medium gray base coat. Use sea sponge to apply dark gray, black, and metallic copper. Speck with more black paint.

MARBLED FAUX FINISHES

Several types of minerals, including serpentine, onyx, alabaster, and breccia, have a marbled or veined appearance and exist in nature in a wide variety of colors. These looks can be duplicated in paint finishes, using a technique called *veining* combined with other techniques.

For the veining, acrylic extender and acrylic thickener are used alongside the paint to create veins that fluctuate from opaque to translucent. A feather is used in an irregular, trembling motion to apply the veins.

Faux onyx (below) resembles the black-and-white onyx rock that is related to marble. Banded areas of chalky white are overlayed on a black background and outlined with white veins.

Faux alabaster has the white, translucent appearance of alabaster, often used for carved vases and ornaments. To achieve alabaster's subtle effect, a base coat of white low-luster enamel is veined with soft gray craft acrylic paint. The entire surface is then whitewashed with diluted paint and softly dry-brushed.

Faux breccia has the irregular, random appearance of real breccia, which is composed of various fragmented rocks, sometimes including marble. Although the painting technique is similar to that of faux alabaster, faux breccia has a bolder look, with areas of peach outlined in gray veining to contrast with the white background. For a more fragmented look, specks of gray are scattered lightly over the surface. On accessories, the veining can be closely spaced and several peach areas can be applied. When using faux breccia on large surfaces like walls, use less veining and space the peach areas farther apart.

Faux serpentine has the variegated dark-green color of the mineral serpentine, as well as its mottled appearance and veins of white. This look is achieved by applying a blend of greens with a sponge in an up-and-down stippling motion, then adding the veins with a feather.

151

HOW TO APPLY A FAUX SERPENTINE PAINT FINISH

MATERIALS

- Black craft acrylic or flat latex paint, for base coat.
- Craft acrylic paints in dark hunter green, medium green, light blue-green, and white; purchase craft acrylic paints in squeeze bottles for easier application.
- Acrylic paint thickener.
- Acrylic paint extender.

- Sponge applicator or synthetic-bristle paintbrush.
- Natural sea sponge.
- Turkey or pheasant feather.
- Disposable plates.
- High-gloss aerosol clear acrylic sealer.

1 Prepare surface (page 120). Apply base coat of black acrylic or flat latex paint. Allow to dry.

2 Squeeze dark hunter green, medium green, and light blue-green paints in random spiraling lines onto disposable plate, overlapping the paint colors.

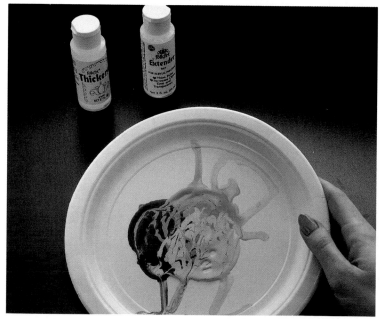

3 Squeeze spiraling lines of thickener and extender over green paints. Tilt plate so colors mingle and marbleize.

4 Dip dampened sea sponge into marbleized green paint; blot lightly onto paper towel to remove excess paint.

5 Dab sponge lightly and repeatedly onto black base coat in an up-and-down stippling motion, turning sponge for random pattern. Allow some base coat to show, and do not mix paint colors together completely; the thickener and extender help keep the colors separate. Allow to dry.

6 Apply long pools of white and medium green paint onto another disposable plate. Apply pool of thickener on one side of paints and extender on the other.

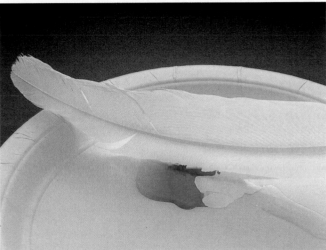

7 Run edge of feather through pools, picking up some thickener, paints, and extender on feather.

8 Place tip of feather onto surface; drag feather along, fidgeting and turning it slightly in your hand to create veins. Apply veins in diagonal direction, crisscrossing them as desired. The thickener and extender vary the veins so some areas are opaque and some are translucent.

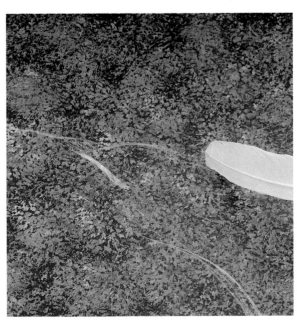

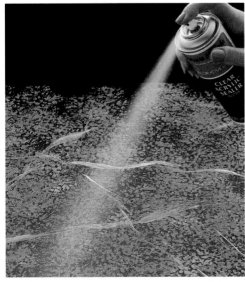

9 Allow paint to dry. Apply several light coats of high-gloss aerosol acrylic sealer.

HOW TO APPLY A FAUX ONYX PAINT FINISH

MATERIALS

- Black craft acrylic or flat latex paint, for base coat.
- White craft acrylic paint.
- Acrylic paint thickener.
- Acrylic paint extender.

- Natural sea sponge.
- Two turkey or pheasant feathers.
- Disposable plate.
- High-gloss aerosol clear acrylic sealer.

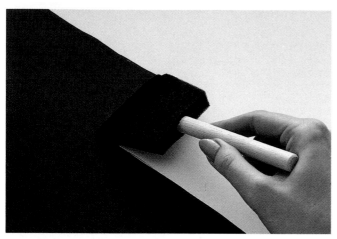

1 Prepare surface (page 120). Apply a base coat of black craft acrylic or flat latex paint. Allow to dry.

2 Apply a long pool of white paint onto a disposable plate. Apply pool of thickener on one side of white paint and extender on the other.

3 Run edge of feather through pools, picking up some thickener, paint, and extender on feather; cover the entire length of feather. Blot excess onto paper towel.

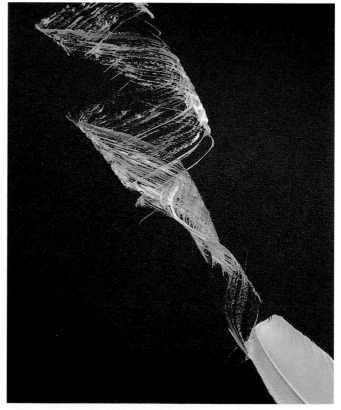

4 Zigzag the feather across base coat in 3" to 4" irregular diagonal bands, with some of the bands meeting or intersecting. Work on only two or three bands at a time, because paint dries quickly.

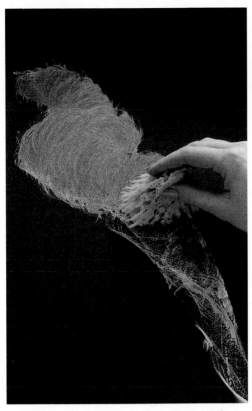

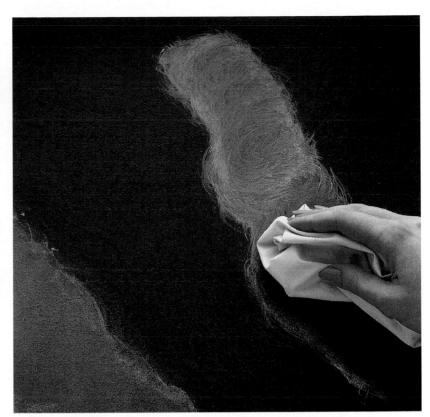

5 Smear the bands of white in a circular motion, using moist sea sponge, for the look of softened light clouds.

6 Rub the bands lightly while still wet, using a dry rag, to give them the appearance of dust on a chalkboard; do not rub over the black base coat. Reapply white paint if too much is rubbed away. If surface dries too quickly, apply water, then rub with rag to soften. Allow to dry.

7 Run edge of the feather through pools of thickener, paint, and extender; blot on paper towel. Place tip of feather onto surface; drag the feather along, fidgeting it and turning it slightly in your hand to create veins. Outline chalky bands with veins; apply more veins in a diagonal direction, crisscrossing them as desired. The thickener and extender vary the veins so some areas are opaque and some are translucent. Allow paint to dry. Apply several coats of high-gloss aerosol clear acrylic sealer.

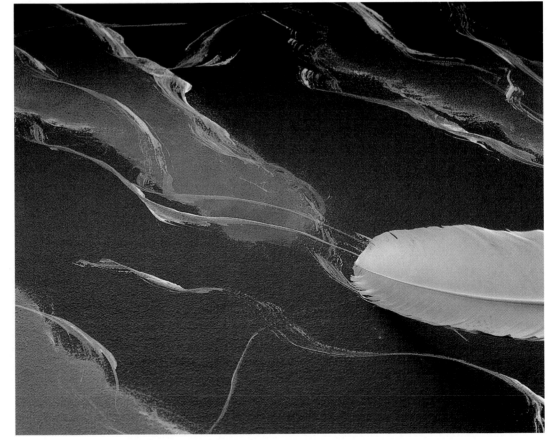

HOW TO APPLY A FAUX ALABASTER PAINT FINISH

MATERIALS

- White low-luster latex enamel paint, for the base coat.
- White craft acrylic or flat latex paint, for the wash.
- Light gray craft acrylic paint, for the veining.
- Acrylic paint thickener.
- Acrylic paint extender.
- Turkey or pheasant feather.
- Disposable plate.
- High-gloss aerosol clear acrylic sealer.

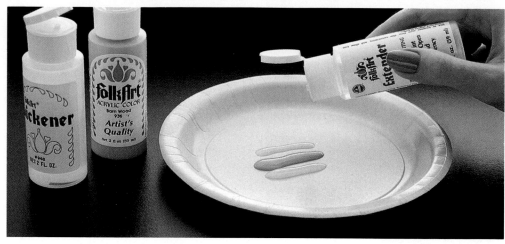

1 Prepare surface (page 120). Apply base coat of white low-luster latex enamel. Allow to dry. Apply a long pool of light gray craft acrylic paint onto disposable plate. Apply a pool of thickener on one side of white paint and extender on the other.

2 Run edge of a feather through pools, picking up some thickener, paint, and extender on feather. Place tip of feather onto surface; drag feather along, fidgeting and turning it slightly in your hand to create veins. Apply veins in a diagonal direction, crisscrossing the veins as desired. The thickener and extender vary the veins so some areas are opaque and some are translucent.

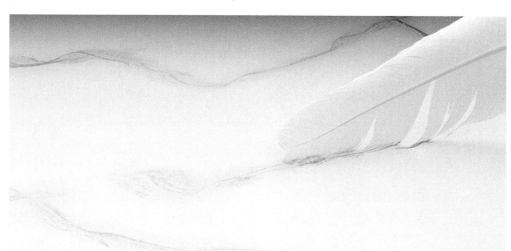

3 Dilute one part white craft acrylic or flat latex paint with one part water, for the wash; brush over surface generously. Before the wash is completely dry, brush the surface diagonally in both directions, using a soft, dry natural-bristle paintbrush, to soften the look.

4 Allow paint to dry. Apply several coats of high-gloss aerosol clear acrylic sealer.

HOW TO APPLY A FAUX BRECCIA PAINT FINISH

MATERIALS

- White low-luster latex enamel paint, for base coat.
- Light gray or medium gray craft acrylic paint, for veining and specking.
- Burnt sienna craft acrylic paint, for the wash.
- Acrylic paint thickener.
- Acrylic paint extender.

- Natural sea sponge; turkey or pheasant feather.
- ½" (1.3 cm) synthetic-bristle flat artist's brush.
- Fine-bristle scrub brush or toothbrush, for specking.
- Disposable plates; small containers.
- High-gloss aerosol clear acrylic sealer.

1 Follow step 1, opposite. Following directions for veining in step 2, opposite, apply veins in diagonal direction, crisscrossing them, and leaving football-shaped areas between veins. Allow to dry.

2 Prepare a wash by mixing one part burnt sienna acrylic paint, two parts acrylic extender, and two parts water.

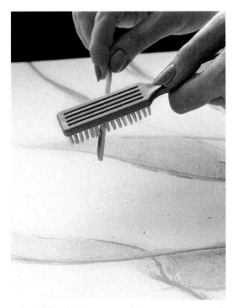

3 Apply the wash to any football-shaped areas between veins, using ½" flat artist's brush. Before the wash is completely dry, blot it with a small, dampened sea sponge, to mottle the finish and remove any brush marks. If the wash spreads outside the veins, wipe it off immediately, using a dampened rag.

4 Add a light to moderate amount of specking as on page 149, using diluted gray craft acrylic paint. Allow the paint to dry. Apply several coats of high-gloss aerosol clear acrylic sealer.

Index